THE AUTHOR

Barry Coughlan was born in Cork and educated at Presentation Brothers College primary and secondary schools. After studying business in the Cork College of Commerce for a year, he joined the then Cork Examiner in 1972 as a trainee reporter. Though primarily a news reporter in the early stages of his career, Barry covered various sports, and mainly rugby, as well. In 1981 he was appointed Rugby Correspondent and since then has travelled extensively, reporting on the Heineken European Cup, the Six Nations Championship, all four World Cup tournaments as well as several overseas international tours. This year he covered his fourth Lions tour for the Irish Examiner when the Four Home Nations team travelled to Australia.

i

Front cover photograph shows Brian "Waltzing" O'Driscoll surging past Australian players Joe Roff (left) and Owen Finegan (on ground) on his way to scoring a spectacular try in the first Test against the Wallabies in Brisbane (Billy Stickland, Inpho).

Back cover photograph shows Tim Horan in action against Ireland in the 1991 World Cup quarter final (Des Barry, Irish Examiner).

THE IRISH LIONS
1896-2001

SFC LIONS BOOKS

First Published 2001 by
SFC Books

© Barry Coughlan 2001

ISBN 0 907085 68 7

Printed by Litho Press,
Roxborough, Midleton, Co. Cork, Ireland.
Tel: 021-4631401

FOR STEPHEN

CONTENTS

ACKNOWLEDGEMENTS

The Irish Lions 1896-2001 was a labour of love rather than a chore. Irish captains, coaches, managers and foot soldiers abound in the long, proud, history of the Lions, and in 1983 I felt it was time that contribution was recognised.

Ireland has provided more captains than any of the other three nations since 1910 and has had influence beyond that through the provision of high profile managers and coaches as rugby has progressed through the years.

For many years the Lions were known as the British Lions and that gave scant credit to Ireland's massive contribution, not to mention the fact that this title caused a great deal of annoyance to many people in this country.

Happily, through the good offices of certain people – amongst them Syd Millar (Chairman of the Four Home Unions) and Donal Lenihan (Manager of the 2001 Lions) - the team is now known as the British and Irish Lions.

In this book, an updated version of the Irish Lions 1896-1983, I dwell mainly on the Irish players and other personnel who have helped create a rugby team that has done the northern hemisphere proud over more than a century.

Many people have helped me in the production.

Heineken Ireland, apart from sponsorship of the title, was fantastically supportive through Heineken Brand Manager Shane Hoyne and Consultant Marketing expert Des McGahan.

Many current and former Irish players – as well as some from England, Scotland and Wales too – have helped by providing information and photographs.

The pictorial content of the 1983 book was limited and I felt it was necessary to expand this section in the 2001 version.

Billy Stickland of Inpho, a top sports photographic agency in Dublin, has covered a number of Lions tours including the most recent one to Australia. Billy took most of the modern-day photographs in the book, including the dramatic front cover picture of

Brian O'Driscoll. I thank him for his professional approach and the top quality photographs he produced.

Des Barry, the award winning Irish Examiner photographer, also provided a number of excellent photographs that have enhanced this production and I offer him my thanks as well.

The Irish Rugby Football Union, through Chief Executive Philip Browne, past President Eddie Coleman and 2001-2002 President Roy Lougheed were very helpful, while archivist Willow Murray spent a considerable amount of time helping me to choose old photographs from his own personal files. I thank him kindly.

The proprietor, Bill O'Callaghan, and staff at Litho Press were hugely helpful, particularly Suzanne O'Shea and Cathy O'Mahony. From a basic plan, Cathy was instrumental in the design of the front cover with some help and fine tuning from my colleague in the Irish Examiner, Der Ahern.

Always lurking in the background was Des McGahan, who spent endless hours advising, cajoling, negotiating, discussing … and demanding action!

May I thank my friends and colleagues in the Irish Examiner for constant encouragement and, of course, my family for allowing me the necessary breathing space when locked away to finalise the production in the Ring Gaeltacht, County Waterford, after returning from the Lions tour.

Barry Coughlan

September 2001

MESSAGE FROM HEINEKEN

Padraic Liston,
Managing Director, Heineken Ireland

Heineken is proud to sponsor the Irish Lions Book 1896 – 2001 following a hugely exciting and action packed year in Irish rugby. The Irish Lions played with great flair and distinction throughout the Tour and created some glorious crowd-pleasing rugby moments for everyone to remember.

Rugby is a high-powered game – fast becoming one of the most popular sports in the world and Heineken is the world's most international beer brand. The synergies that exist between the two will benefit both Irish Rugby and its supporters for many seasons to come.

Heineken is proud of its contribution to the development of rugby in Ireland from grass roots level to the prestigious Heineken Cup, the top Club and Province tournament in Europe and Heineken Kinsale 7's which offers top class 7's rugby and a great social weekend in the picturesque town of Kinsale. Heineken has invested heavily in Irish Rugby over the last number of years and will maintain its commitment to the sport for many years to come.

Barry Coughlan, in his beautifully presented account of the Irish Team on the Lions Tour, gives us a colourful insight into what it means to be an Irishman on such a Tour. From the great figures of the past like Ronnie Dawson and Willie John McBride through to the latter day heroics of Keith Wood, Brian O'Driscoll and Rob

Henderson, Barry places the reader firmly at the centre of the action and excitement.

Irish involvement in the Lions has never been stronger and there is a special focus on this year's tour to Australia when the greatest players from these islands assembled under one flag to face the world champions. Whether it's the sweet potential of that first balmy victory in Brisbane or the defiant last stand at Sydney's Stadium Australia, the reader will delight in the first-hand experience of this most unique of sporting events.

Managing Director, Heineken Ireland

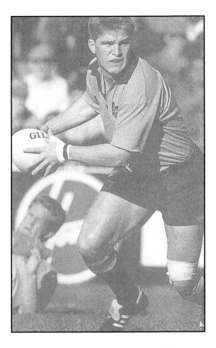

FOREWORD
BY TIM HORAN

I am delighted and deem it a great honour to write the foreword for this book to celebrate the contribution made by Irish players to Lions tours over many years.

There are a number of reasons why I was happy to do so – not least because I have played a lot of Test rugby and appreciate the sacrifices one has to make to reach the top, particularly in the amateur days of old.

I would have to say, however, that the main reason was because I wanted to be party to this tribute to Irish rugby and its players.

Having been on many tours with Australia, I can say unequivocally that Ireland was the favourite country I visited because of the hospitality I received from the people, either those involved in rugby or otherwise.

As a youngster in Australia, I can remember looking at a rugby video, 101 Best Tries. Many of them stuck out but I can never forget one in particular, scored by Mike Gibson.

On my first tour, in the company of such established players as Michael Lynagh and Nick Farr-Jones, I remember we went to a school to chat with some youngsters. It was organised by Ollie Campbell, another famous Irish player, and I can only say I was delighted to be involved.

Imagine my surprise, later into the trip, when I got to meet Mike Gibson and was even invited back to his house for a cup of hot chocolate and a chat.

These are some of the things I will remember all of my life, long after my rugby career is finished. I have great memories of Ireland – not just because I have Irish ancestors – but because of the hospitality I received and friendships I made.

During the World Cup of 1991, the Australian squad was based in the Westbury Hotel off Grafton Street in Dublin. In those days we were not paid and the squad still like to go out and have a drink up.

We took to the streets selling t-shirts to make a bit of money for ourselves. The fund we set up was really for "party money" but it also gave us an opportunity to meet more of the people of Ireland, people who had little or no interest in rugby.

I reckon people took us to their hearts but we took them to ours too because they were so nice to us during that time and in 1999 when we stayed out in Portmarnock.

People in other countries are hospitable too, of course, but I just feel that hospitality in Ireland flows more freely than anywhere else.

I should, I suppose, point out that many Australians believe we won both World Cups because we were based in Ireland!

One of the things I like about Irish rugby is the ease with which the game has progressed from the amateur to professional eras.

Every noted rugby playing country has suffered in a bid to keep the amateur game alive, to ensure that the grass roots continue to be held in high esteem. From what I can see, Ireland has done it better than anyone else in difficult circumstances.

On the international front, Ireland has come a long way in the last couple of years. Last season, they made a big impact on the Six Nations Championship and had shown signs of doing that for a while before.

The recent Lions tour was proof of the strength of Irish rugby. Ireland provided Keith Wood, Brian O'Driscoll and Rob Henderson to the Test side and I have no hesitation in saying that, along with Richard Hill, these were the best group of players in the party.

Without any of these three, the Lions would not have won the first Test or gone so close to winning the third and the series.

The other Irish players in the party may not have made the same impact but there were still good performances. It should be remembered that this was a particularly short tour for a team like the Lions to come together, but if the remaining Irishmen didn't win Test places, none of them let the squad down.

The fact that so many of them made the tour suggests strongly that Irish rugby has a good future. I know that Irish players have always had a big influence on Lions tours and many of them have become household names in world rugby.

This is a golden opportunity for Ireland to build on the recent success by utilising the current crop of top quality players as role models for the youngsters of the country.

If I could give any advice to Ireland it would be this; bring on more youngsters while role models such as Brian O'Driscoll, Keith Wood and Rob Henderson are still involved at the top level. It is much easier to introduce young players to an environment where they can look up to such high quality people rather than wait until they are gone.

I know that rugby in Ireland is strong at under-age levels. The country has produced top class schools, under 19 and under 21 teams in recent years. If that success, and it appears to be about to happen, can be translated into high achievement with the national team, then the future is very bright.

One thing I should suggest is that outright success will not necessarily be achieved by hard work alone. Some of the spontaneity; some of the fun appears to have gone out of rugby.

Ironically, that may have been the very reason why the Lions failed to beat Australia in the 2001 series. Whilst I sympathised with their plight of having to bring a team from four nations together in such a short space of time, I think they maybe concentrated too much on hard work to the detriment of other essential ingredients that make a rugby player and a successful rugby team.

Enjoyment is imperative if players are to get the best from themselves and from others. Maybe the 2001 Lions, whilst being a very professional, dedicated and hard working squad that went agonisingly close to winning the series did not enjoy themselves as much as they should and, perhaps, lessons can be learned from that for the future.

CHAPTER 1

THE HISTORY OF THE LIONS

THE players lucky enough to win selection on a Lions squad will readily admit the honour to be the pinnacle of their careers. Equally, the fans in Australia, New Zealand and South Africa look forward to such tours with unprecedented excitement.

In short, the rugby fraternity believe there is nothing quite like the Lions, a blended team comprised of English, Irish, Welsh and Scotsmen who now come together every four years to undertake a major overseas tour.

In bygone days, Australia was a happy hunting ground but in the previously more dodgy territories of New Zealand and South Africa, success was hard to come by.

In 1971, the Lions finally came good against the All Blacks when Welshman John Dawes captained them to their first series win. Three years later, Willie John McBride led the Lions to a smashing victory run over the Springboks and in 1997, Martin Johnson's squad, with the help of four Irishmen, shocked everyone by winning the series 2-1 against the then World Champions.

It was only the second time the Lions had managed to beat South Africa in a series since their tours became official in 1910.

1

Win or lose, however, the Lions attract huge attention from the media and the public. They are the team everyone wants to play against and that everyone wants to see.

Well known New Zealand journalist T. P. McLean once wrote about them: "It is curious that great matches played by the Lions on their tours to this country since 1950 are easier to remember than some of the memorable achievements by the All Blacks and of other teams playing against them."

In New Zealand and South Africa in particular, where Rugby Union rules over all other sports, the Lions have a magnetic attraction. And while rugby has more competition from other codes in Australia, the emergence of the Wallabies to win the World Cup in both 1991 and 1999 has helped give the game a much bigger profile than in the past.

The Lions bring out the crowds and are a major money-spinner for the host Union, even if the length of their tours has been significantly cut over the years.

The Lions have a unique policy of never playing at home, although in special circumstances they did so officially on one occasion in Cardiff in 1986.

Supporters in Britain and Ireland, save for those lucky enough to join the ever-increasing numbers of supporters groups, follow their movements on foreign soil with avid interest. Newspaper, radio and particularly television coverage has never been greater than in the last decade.

The future of the Lions appears to be assured despite the increased pressures brought to bear since the game became professional.

In 1977, the Lions played 26 games on a tour to New Zealand and Fiji. Three and six years later, in South Africa and New Zealand respectively, they played 18 times including four Tests, the norm at that time.

When Finlay Calder led the Lions on their 1989 tour to Australia, the list of matches was cut to 12 - with three Tests against the Wallabies and one against a composite team of Australians and New Zealanders called the Anzacs.

That smaller itinerary was due at the time to the fact that Australia was not in a position to provide enough quality opposition beyond the internationals and teams such as Queensland, New South Wales and ACT. The one lightweight team the Lions met was New South Wales Country and the result of that (72-13) tells its own story.

Even then, there was a change of thinking. Previous tours were deemed to be too long and the decision was made, in any event, to restrict them.

That appeared to work against them in 1993 when Gavin Hastings brought a team back to New Zealand. There were just 13 games and most of them were, apart from the Tests, against the top provincial sides in that country. The biggest midweek victory was against Taranaki (49-25) and the Lions lost to Otago, Auckland, Hawkes Bay and Waikato as well as the Test series.

The first professional Lions squad was in 1997 and, happily, the shortened itinerary didn't unduly bother them. They returned with a rare series victory and lost just one of the provincial games - to Northern Transvaal.

The old days when Lions players had to request time off from work and exist on a daily allowance for out of pocket expenses are well and truly over.

Now they are highly paid professionals playing with the full blessing of their employers at a time of the year when the clubs, provinces or countries can do without their services.

There is no scrimping or saving, no begging and imploring companies around Britain and Ireland to continue paying the wages so that families can survive.

In the amateur days of 1983, for instance, players were given a tour allowance of £8 a day. Now, they have potential earnings of £28,000 sterling and are guaranteed a minimum of £15,000 sterling for seven weeks work.

Effectively, they don't have to put their hands in the pocket. All travel, five star accommodation and food is paid for. Each player is supplied with a wide range of clothing. They don't even have to pay to telephone home because they are supplied with mobile telephones and laptop computers.

According to Tour Manager Donal Lenihan: "They will want for nothing. They will have more gear and equipment than is available in a superstore. And most of their wives and partners will be around for part of the tour!"

Although the 1997 tour of South Africa was a turning point in the history of the Lions, the 2001 trip to Australia was arguably the single biggest undertaking.

Once restricted to a party of 30 players, 35 started the tour to South Africa and 37 to Australia.

The selection process began a short time after the appointment of Donal Lenihan in February 2000. He was widely tipped to get the post and backed in his bid to get it by Fran Cotton, the Englishman who headed the squad to South Africa.

One of his main jobs was to seek out the services of a coaching team on behalf of the Four Home Unions and it was clear that the preference was to appoint Ian McGeechan whose track record in 1989, 1993 and 1997 was exemplary.

McGeechan, despite repeated attempts to get him on board, felt it was time to step aside and concentrate instead on his job as Scottish coach. Lenihan negotiated with him over a period of two months before finally accepting McGeechan's decision to stick with Scotland.

So the approach was made to Graham Henry, a New Zealander who had been brought in to coach Wales.

Henry's experience and success as a coach had been immense but he had been unable to turn Wales back into the super power the Welsh fans craved for.

Additionally, there was some shock that the Lions would turn, for the very first time, to an outsider.

Still, Henry's appointment was welcomed too. He was clearly the best of the other candidates and his knowledge of southern hemisphere rugby was deemed to be a major factor.

Lenihan was up-front with Henry and informed him of his negotiations with McGeechan. From day one, Henry knew he was second choice but relished the opportunity of what was sure to be the biggest challenge of his coaching career.

The manager had then, of course, to meet with the Welsh Rugby Union and discuss the matter with them. He had to come up with a set of proposals to assure the Union that Henry would be able to combine both jobs without the national team suffering.

Andy Robinson, former English international with coaching experience at Bath and with England, was chosen by Lenihan to act as forwards coach to assist McGeechan. Now, with a change, he discussed the appointment with Henry who was happy to act on Lenihan's advice and Robinson was brought on board in the middle of June 2000, just after England returned from a tour to South Africa.

From there on, they worked in close co-operation with four selection advisors, John O'Driscoll (Ireland), Simon Halliday (England), John Rutherford (Scotland) and Derek Quinnell (Wales) as they set about the huge task. All four men were in place by September, ready to assess player performances from the start of the Heineken European Cup.

Having watched over 100 matches, with particular emphasis on individual players, the selectors released a preliminary squad of 67 names early in 2001. As events transpired, just one player from outside that group, England's Jason Robinson, made the final cut of 37.

Ultimately, the selection group attended more than 200 games although their job can't cave been helped by the postponement of Ireland's Six Nations ties against England, Scotland and Wales due to the Foot and Mouth disease which struck in Britain in the Spring.

Perhaps their plans were not as badly affected as they might in the amateur days when politics was very much a part of selection but there is no doubt that a couple of Irishmen probably lost out and a couple of Welsh players gained as a result of the spread of the disease.

Many people ask about the historical background to the title - the Lions - this four nation's team have been given.

It goes back almost 80 years. By then, New Zealand had been nicknamed the All Blacks and South Africa had become known as the Springboks.

When a British and Irish side went to South Africa in 1924, the symbol they used was that of a Lion, the same as one used by a British military regiment. The South African press corps, anxious to add colour to the occasion, picked up on it and since then they have been known as the Lions.

Today they wear scarlet jerseys, white shorts and navy stockings with a green turnover, representing the colours of the four home unions.

It was not always the case, however. The first touring sides wore red, white and blue striped jerseys, white shorts and red stockings. The colours were later changed to blue jerseys, white shorts and red stockings, but before the 1930 tour to New Zealand the Irish protested and a green elasticised flash was added to the hose.

That outfit, significantly, was greeted with equal howls of protest from New Zealand who then had to play in white for the Test matches, thus becoming known briefly as the All Whites.

After the setting up of the four home unions committee in 1949, the Lions travelled to New Zealand a year later. This time, they were kitted out in the gear that remains identified with them to the present day, despite modern modifications in jersey design and the inclusion of sponsors' logos.

CHAPTER 2

RUGBY IN IRELAND

RUGBY is played in well over 100 countries throughout the world in some form or another, and 82 of those countries are now affiliated to the International Rugby Board.

When talking about rugby, most people tend to think of the obvious - Ireland, England, Scotland, Wales, France, New Zealand, South Africa, Australia, Argentina, Italy, Canada, Romania, Fiji, Western Samoa and maybe the USA.

It is a game which has a much broader base than that, although it may take years more to take a proper foothold in developing nations.

Andorra is one of the world's smallest participants with just a couple of clubs and 150 players. Others, like Liberia and Malawi, with 400 players between them, are never likely to be anything other than a dot on the rugby landscape.

Countries like Thailand, South Korea and Belgium have all shown increases in numbers playing the game in the last decade. Indeed, the Thai Rugby Union, mindful of the view that Asia and particularly China has immense potential for expansion and development, is actively promoting the establishment of an Asian Five Nations competition similar to the Six Nations competition involving the big guns of Europe and to the Tri Nations in the southern hemisphere.

It may come as a surprise to know that in Fiji, a group of islands with a combined population of about 600,000, there are almost as many people playing rugby as in Ireland which has a population base seven times greater.

Japan, hardly one of the world's rugby super powers, has, nevertheless, more than six times the number of adult players available for national selection than Ireland. It will be interesting to monitor Japan's progress in the coming few years, following a recent decision to go professional and the appointment of two full time overseas coaches.

The top 60 players in the country have been contracted by the JRFU and will, in future, spend six months between March and August in full time training and involved in an increased schedule of matches.

Before the break up of Russia, over 60,000 people played the game there. The numbers have grown in the fledgling countries since then.

Ireland, according to recent IRB figures, has 16,000 senior players and a total of 65,000 at all levels. The figures have increased significantly in the last 20 years and compare favourably to countries like Canada (total of 30,000), Italy (27,000), Wales (62,000) and Scotland (48,000).

But when compared to the Japanese total of 150,000 and especially to long established and highly successful rival nations England (1.3 million), South Africa (303,000), France (270,000), New Zealand (125,000) and Australia (108,000), it becomes clear that Ireland has done very well to have earned the respect it enjoys in the world of rugby.

In general, the last 20 years have not been good in terms of Ireland's international record. Notwithstanding Triple Crown victories in 1982 and 1985 as well as a good year in 1983, Ireland has lost ground to all but Wales in the Five Nations.

The last two, since the addition of Italy to form a Six Nations tournament, have shown signs of an improvement. At last, Ireland has beaten France and Scotland after horrible runs without victory.

To date, Ireland's percentage record in the championship is just over 40 per cent. Against individual countries it reads; against England 37.5 per cent, France 40 per cent, Wales 40 per cent, Scotland 44 per cent and Italy 100 per cent.

The Irish Rugby Football Union was founded in Dublin in 1874 and, since it did not include Belfast, a different Union was formed north of the border. Yet when Ireland first played England at the Oval in 1875 there were four Ulstermen present. Four years later the rift was healed and the bodies joined together.

Two years later they met Scotland for the first time. It was the first international played in Belfast and it was a rather forgettable experience from the Irish point of view, for they lost the game by six goals and two tries to nothing.

These results - or losses - were to haunt Ireland in their games against both England and Scotland for the remainder of the century.

It should be remembered England, for instance, only lost to Ireland twice in the first 20 meetings between the countries up to the start of the 20th Century. Scotland dished out much of the same treatment with Ireland managing just two three wins and three draws in the first 20. Wales also steamed ahead in those formative years of the championship, although not by as much. They won 12 and drew one of the first 20 with Ireland winning seven times.

It was the opposite against France who only joined the competition in 1909 and who struggled in the early years. Ireland won 14 of the first 20, but history shows that it took victory in Paris the season before last to end a losing sequence of 15 games.

The statistics show that Ireland finished each of the last two centuries badly. They started each of the two new ones on a much higher note!

Still, for all of Ireland's bad patches, the country is still highly regarded throughout the world as a relatively powerful rugby nation.

It is generally acknowledged that the Irish have a great feel, a tremendous passion for the game. Something draws us to the excitement of the international arena, and something in our nature spurs us to overcome difficult obstacles. All over the world, in green or red Lions' jerseys, the Irish have won great respect.

Tom Kiernan was one of the greatest administrators in the history of the game until his recent retirement. He played for Ireland 54 times. He captained the Irish team and the Lions, he coached Munster to an historic win over New Zealand in 1978 and in 1982 was coach when Ireland turned back the clock 33 years to win the Triple Crown.

In relation to the bigger rugby nations, Kiernan acknowledges Ireland's difficulties in producing good teams on a consistent basis.

"Yes, we have problems in doing that but I believe we produce players with basic qualities comparable to or better than some of the others. Irish sportsmen in general are more realistic and honest, and they have a better attitude. They are often more loyal than players from other nations."

All countries produce stars and characters that became known worldwide, some of whom legends.

In the context of Ireland, Louis Magee, "Blucher" Doran, the Ryan Brothers Mick and Jack, Mossy Landers, Jammy Clinch, Eugene Davy, Jack Kyle, Karl Mullen, J. C. Daly, Tom Clifford, Tony O'Reilly, Ronnie Dawson, Dave Hewitt, Bill Mulcahy, Noel Murphy, Jerry Walsh, Kiernan himself, Mike Gibson, Syd Millar, Willie John McBride, Fergus Slattery, Willie Duggan, Moss Keane, Ollie Campbell, Tony Ward, Ciaran Fitzgerald, Donal Lenihan, Brendan Mullin, Nick Popplewell, Keith Wood, Mick Galwey and Peter Clohessy slip easily into the legend category for various reasons.

There were, are and will be many more.

A decade ago, at the inaugural World Sevens Cup in Edinburgh, Ireland reached the semi-final against all the odds, and lost in injury time to a star-studded Australian side.

Consequently, they were recipients of a special award for the best unseeded team in the tournament. But the Irish, in those amateur days, were unable to wait the extra day for the award to be presented at a gala lunch.

I was the only Irishman present and was asked to receive the award on behalf of the squad. Shyness got the better of me and I decided against going on stage in front of 450 people. Instead, Scottish captain Gavin Hastings agreed to receive the trophy.

Hastings, in a very brief address, noted: "The Irish turn up in your face when least expected and they don't turn up when you expect them to. They are as unpredictable off the pitch as they are on it!"

One individual Irish legend was Ernie Crawford, the man credited with bringing the word "Alickadoo" into the rugby vocabulary.

The term evidently originated when Crawford got annoyed with a colleague for being more interested in reading a book about the Orient than in joining a card game.

Crawford snarled angrily at him: "Bloody Ali Khadu!"

Subsequently, anyone who did not match up to Crawford's expectations was similarly berated and today the word is commonly used to describe the non-playing members of clubs, men whose functions may or may not be exactly defined.

The late Jammie Clinch was another of the old brigade who made no secret of the admiration he had for the new breed of player in the pre-professional era. He was a regular visitor to Ireland's training sessions prior to international games in Dublin but he didn't suffer fools gladly.

One of the Irish players who had missed a tackle in an international prior to one visit to a training camp was pointed out: "See him, he's nothing but a coward!"

11

Anyone shirking a tackle was never forgiven, even if it happened only once. Clinch, in the 1920's, was big, exuberant, fun loving and not overly enamoured with following any pre-conceived game plans.

While Crawford would try to out wit his opponents, Clinch didn't hold at all with the notion of going around an obstacle. He preferred to go right through it.

Clinch build such a reputation as a hard man that when he ran onto the pitch before an international in Cardiff, a Welsh fan screamed: "Send the bastard off ref!"

One of the great exponents of ball control on the ground, the dribble, was Tom Clifford who made such a lasting impression on everyone when selected for the 1950 Lions tour to New Zealand.

It is a measure of the innocence of those times that before his departure from Limerick, his mother baked a number of large cakes for him to eat during the long voyage, thinking her son would be hungry.

It is a measure of the way in which these stories gather momentum that his colleagues still say today he had a special ship following the ocean liner to carry all the food he brought with him!

Stories about Tony O'Reilly are endless. His endeavours for the Lions are well documented; 16 tries in South Africa in 1955 (a record), 17 in New Zealand in 1959 (a record he shares with John Bevan who achieved the same number in 1971).

In try scoring terms, he had less success for Ireland, probably because he was always a marked man and possibly because of a recurring shoulder injury that hampered him at various stages of his career.

After playing for Ireland for what appeared to be the last time in 1963, he set about building an international reputation as a businessman. By 1970, amongst other things, he had worked his way up to an appointment of vice-president with Heinz.

That year, Ireland met England at Twickenham and after winger Bill Brown cried off the team, O'Reilly was called upon as a shock replacement.

He arrived at the match in a manner befitting his business status and found a telegram awaiting him from Johnny Quirke: "Heinz Beanz are Has Beanz."

In 1974, Willie John McBride led the Lions in South Africa and helped them to a famous series victory. McBride, a well-known "wrecker" in his day, but now the exemplary captain, was still ready for a challenge to his sense of good humour.

There had been some misbehaviour (a regular happening on Lions tours in those days) by some of the players in the team hotel one evening.

According to McBride: "Ah, there was some messing going on in a corridor. Someone had spilled drink, broken a door and someone else had a fire hose or something."

The manager of the hotel was unimpressed and challenged the culprits. After warning them to behave, the answers he got were less than satisfactory and so he stormed off, threatening to call the police.

At that very moment, McBride stepped from the lift, the manager stopped in his tracks and informed the Irishman of his intentions.

In a strong South African accent, he screamed: "I vill call the police." McBride looked stunned for a moment before turning to ask: "And tell me sir, how many of them vill there be?"

Moss Keane may have learned some of the tricks of the trade from McBride when he packed down with him ten times for Ireland in 1974 and 1975 but Keane certainly didn't need any lessons in comedy.

Keane played against France in 1982 and was charging towards the line for what seemed to be a certain try. Just as he was about to get the touchdown, a French player hit him from the side and the ball popped from his grasp.

13

Later, as he explained the moment, Keane claimed he had done it deliberately: "Well, it was like this: I was over the line when all of a sudden I remembered Willie John had scored against France in his last international. Had I scored, it might have meant the end of my career so I threw the ball away!"

Fergus Slattery, Ireland's long-serving flanker, was around long enough to build up a dossier of stories on several players.

One of his favourites concerned Willie Duggan when he played an exhibition match in South Africa 20 odd years ago.

Duggan wasn't particularly interested in the game, having enjoyed the South African hospitality over the previous few days. Finally, he retired in a state of exhaustion. When another player was tackled into touch nearby a couple of minutes later, he noticed Duggan grinding his heel into the turf. Curious, he asked what Duggan was doing. The response was lightning: "I have been following this damn snail around all afternoon and I've finally caught up with him!"

Ireland's competitive edge has never been blunt, even if success in terms of Triple Crowns and the Championship has been rare. The Irish revel in the role of "underdog", and in that situation they very often defy the critics.

Interest in the game is growing all the time. Towns and areas that heretofore were strongholds of other sports, notably GAA, have produced clubs to take their place amongst the senior ranks.

The All Ireland leagues, introduced a decade ago, have helped the spread of the game and still have a role to play in the development of Irish rugby, despite a more troubled history in the last few seasons since the advent of professionalism and the extension of provincial rugby into Europe.

It would be fair to say that the Irish Rugby Football Union have, in general, dealt with professionalism very well.

Initially, it was an all hell breaking loose situation. The influence of English clubs as they snapped up the services of Ireland's top players for big money threatened to wreck the structure of the game here.

The vision displayed by those in recognising a three-tiered system (club, province and country) was to be welcomed and it was the way forward. The Union created four strong provincial squads to compete in the Heineken European Cup. This has borne fruit.

Ulster won the European Cup in 1999. Munster were finalists in 2000 and semi-finalists last season. They lost both games, to Northampton and Stade Francais respectively, by a mere point. Leinster have enjoyed significant success in the tournament as well, while Connacht, even though struggling for the last couple of seasons, have the capacity to do better.

In that sense, Ireland has embraced professionalism well. It has come about through a determined stance by top IRFU officials who have created a solid structure. Good management, quality coaches and the ability to learn from mistakes made elsewhere, particularly in England, has also helped.

Players once domiciled in Britain are drifting home. The tide has turned and the Irish are no longer to be trifled with on the field of play. The new Millennium could be the start of a bright new dawn.

There have been changes too at grass roots level, some good, and some bad. Clubs, particularly the major ones, have every reason not to be happy with the way the game has gone. The emergence of the provinces as a major force has undoubtedly left them in a weakened position, some financially and others on the field of play.

It is to be hoped that some time in the not too distant future, the Irish Rugby Football Union come up with a satisfactory formula to accommodate the clubs properly within the new structure.

The decision some years ago to offer junior clubs a facility to break into the big time has, however, been a stunning success. It is, of course, sad to see long established senior clubs drop out of the All Ireland League but that is the price one must pay for progress.

The positive side of this is that it has helped spread the game throughout the country. The power base rested for too long in the cities, sometimes in clubs with little or no community involvement.

That has changed significantly and it is a major step forward. Clubs like Ballynahinch, the Connemara All Blacks, Naas, Barnhall, Midleton and Clonakilty have joined the senior ranks.

It is too early yet to predict how Connemara and Clonakilty will fare, but the others have all been significant players in the All Ireland Leagues. Community spirit, enthusiasm and progressive thinking have given club rugby in Ireland a greater impetus and, undoubtedly, strength.

Total reliance on the schools system is, happily, gone. Rugby in Ireland is far less elitist than it was even just a couple of decades ago. Country teams, with the benefit of that great community spirit, are increasing in number and reaping the rewards as well.

A shining example, quite apart from those who have already made the senior ranks, would be Bruff in County Limerick.

It is a club that thrives on family involvement with a huge membership of 600 in a community that numbers little more than 1000. The under-age section has been hugely successful in the last few years with the under 16's winning an All Ireland league title, the under 18's sharing one and, more recently, the under 20 group emerging successful yet again.

Apart from producing Irish prop forward John Hayes, three of the youth members recently toured Australia with the Irish under 21 squad for the Sanzar tournament.

It all goes to prove that hard work does pay off, and that the game in Ireland is not just spreading but growing in importance as well.

CHAPTER 3

THE EARLY YEARS

Although the English were the touring pioneers, well before the dawning of the 20th century Ireland made a handsome contribution to the success of overseas tours.

It should be pointed out that the first tour - to Australia and New Zealand in 1888 - had the backing of, but was not instigated by, the Rugby Football Union. Indeed many of the players included were not affiliated to the Union and few of those who were there went on to win international honours.

There were no Irishmen in that first touring party, led by Englishman R. L. Seddon who died tragically in a boating accident. The death was an obvious blow to the members of the party, but it did not affect their play. A. E. Stoddard, one of the driving forces behind the tour, took over the captaincy and they returned home in triumph with 27 victories and six draws. They lost only two games - to Auckland and Taranaki on the New Zealand sector of the trip.

1891: SOUTH AFRICA

Three years later, in 1891, another tour party left Britain. This time the Rugby Union was fully in favour of it.

The challenge came from South Africa, and the view within the RFU was that it had to be met.

So it was, and the touring side emerged winners of all 19 games. After conceding one try (then just a single point) in their opening match against the Cape Town Clubs, they kept a clean sheet in all their remaining games – a truly remarkable record. They rattled up a points tally of 223 and "whitewashed" South Africa in the Test series.

1888 RESULTS

Played	Won	Drew	Lost	For	Against
35	27	6	2	300	101

Otago	W 8-3
Otago	W 4-3
Canterbury	W 14-6
Canterbury	W 4-0
Wellington	D 3-3
Roberts XV	W 4-1*
Taranaki	L 0-1*
Auckland	W 6-3
Auckland	L 0-4
New South Wales	W 18-2
Bathurst	W 13-6
New South Wales	W 18-6
Sydney Juniors	W 11-0
King's School	D 10-10
Sydney Grammar	D 3-3
Bathurst	W 20-10
New South Wales	W 16-2
University of Sydney	W 8-4
Newcastle	W 15-7
Queensland	W 13-6
Queensland Juniors	W 11-3
Queensland	W 7-0
Ipswich	W 12-1*
Melbourne	W 15-5
Adelaide	W 28-3
Auckland	W 3-0
Auckland	D 1-1*

Hawkes Bay	W 3-2
Wairarapa	W 5-1*
Canterbury	W 8-0
Otago	D 0-0
South Island	W 5-3
South Island	W 6-0
Taranaki Clubs	W 7-1*
Wanganui	D 1-1*

*Try = 1 point

1891 RESULTS

Played	Won	Drew	Lost	For	Against
19	19	0	0	223	1

Cape Town Clubs	W 15-1*
Western Provinces	W 6-0
Cape Colony	W 14-0
Kimberly	W 7-0
Griqualand West	W 3-0
Port Elizabeth	W 22-0
Eastern Province	W 21-0
SOUTH AFRICA	W 4-0
Grahamstown District	W 9-0
King Williams Town	W 18-0
King Williamstown/Disrict	W 15-0
Natal	W 25-0
Transvaal	W 22-0
Johannesburg	W 15-0
Johannesburg/Pretoria	W 9-0
Cape Colony	W 4-0
SOUTH AFRICA	W 3-0
Cape Colony	W 7-0
SOUTH AFRICA	W 4-0

*Try = 1 point

1896: SOUTH AFRICA

THE emergence of Ireland as a rugby force in 1894 played a significant role in the selection of Irish players for the first time on a four nations overseas tour.

The year was 1896 and those responsible for the selection of the squad could not afford to ignore the fact that Ireland won their first Triple Crown a couple of years before.

Although Scotland won the Triple Crown in 1895, Ireland bounced back strongly to take the 1896 championship and pressed claims for a number of players to make the trip to South Africa.

In percentage terms, it was Ireland's strongest representation ever because nine of the 21 players made it.

One of those to the forefront of that successful season was Tommy Crean of Wanderers and he was to become famous in other aspects of life later on.

While Englishman John Hammond was named as tour captain, Crean had a profound influence on the proceedings. He captained the side in two of the Test matches and in several of the provincial games.

He was quite a character by all accounts and did more than anyone to ensure it was a success.

The touring side played 21 times, won 19 games, drew one and lost one – the last Test against South Africa - after they had wrapped up the series in the first three matches.

Crean received lavish praise in the journals of the time. The South Africans were amazed that a man of his size (he stood 6 feet 2 inches which, at that time, was big) could be so mobile. But Crean was, in fact, a sprint champion who was also so strong that he became almost impossible to stop in full flight. His strength, speed and high knee action made him one of the toughest players of his time.

By the end of the tour, Crean had scored five tries, made many more and built up an enviable reputation as a leader of men. It was no surprise that he should later go on to display his bravery elsewhere.

In those early tours, it was not uncommon for players to remain in the countries they toured. He and club colleague Robert Johnston took advantage of the assisted passage and stayed in South Africa. When the Boer War broke out in 1899, both joined the Imperial Light Horse, an army unit set up in the Transvaal.

Crean worked his way up to the rank of captain and was wounded while helping his unit defend their position At Tygerskloof. He continued on in characteristic fashion to help his fellow soldiers but was struck again which allegedly prompted him to cry out: "By Christ, I'm killed entirely."

But Crean did not die and, for his bravery, he was awarded the Victoria Cross. He went on to fight in World War One and won another medal for bravery before settling down to practice as a doctor in Harley Street.

Johnston did not make as big a reputation for himself on the playing pitches. He had been capped just twice for Ireland, and while he played well in a number of games, did not make the team for the Tests.

In battle, he was as valiant as Crean. He was also a captain in the Imperial Light Horse and helped his unit to win one particular battle against huge odds. For courage beyond the call of duty, he too was awarded the prized Victoria Cross.

Louis Magee had, the season before, established himself as a halfback of exceptional quality on the Irish team. He went on to become one of the best-known Irish internationals and win 28 caps. In that summer of 1896, he won himself new admirers. His brother J.T. Magee, who played in the same side at Bective Rangers, joined him on tour. He never actually got to play rugby for Ireland but was an international cricketer. Yet, in South Africa, he was highly impressive and won his place in the side for two of the Tests.

Another well-known personality on that tour was A.D. Clinch, who played ten times for Ireland. He was father of a future international of note, Jammie Clinch, who was one of the great characters of the game.

Universities rugby was very strong in those days and it was no real surprise that four men from Dublin University were included. L.Q Bulger, J. Sealy, A. D. Meares and C.A. Boyd were the four, and if Bulger and Sealy were the most successful of the group on that tour, the experience gained helped the others go on to play for Ireland. Boyd won three caps between 1900 and 1901 while Mears played four times in 1899 and 1900.

Sealy played nine times for Ireland between 1896 and 1900 and, like Bulger, who also won eight caps, played in all four Tests on tour.

Bulger was the most prolific try scorer in the party. He got in for 20 tries, representing over 30 per cent of the tourists' total of 65.

So it was that Irishmen forged their first links with a team that was later to become known as the Lions.

1896 RESULTS

Played	Won	Drew	Lost	For	Against
21	19	1	1	320	45

Cape Town Clubs	W 14-9
Suburban Clubs	W 8-0
Western Province	D 0-0
Griqualand West	W 11-9
Griqualand West	W 16-0
Port Elizabeth/Uitenhage	W 26-3
Eastern Province	W 18-0
SOUTH AFRICA	W 8-0
Grahamstown	W 20-0
King Williams Town	W 25-0
East London	W 27-0
Queenstown	W 25-0
Johannesburg/Country	W 7-0
Transvaal	W 16-3
Johannesburg/Town	W 18-0
Transvaal	W 16-5
SOUTH AFRICA	W 17-8
Cape Colony	W 7-0
SOUTH AFRICA	W 9-3
Western Province	W 32-0
SOUTH AFRICA	L 0-5

1899: AUSTRALIA

Tom McGown had the distinction of becoming the first player from a Northern Ireland club to tour abroad with a British and Irish side.

He was one of three Irishmen selected on the team to tour Australia, a trip that was unique in the history of the Lions until 1989.

It was the first and last time – until Clive Rowlands and Finlay Calder brought a side to Australia 12 years ago – to tour that country without also visiting New Zealand.

The records of that particular tour are rather scant, but it seems strange that only McGown (NIFC), E. Martelli (Dublin University) and G. P. Doran (Lansdowne) made the tour because Ireland had dominated the home internationals that season.

They won the Triple Crown for the second time and both Doran and McGown were there to help them do it. Martelli appeared to come from nowhere – another of the players in those early days who never won a cap for their own country, yet toured abroad with the four nations.

Doran went on to have a distinguished international career and won eight caps while McGown, though not faring as well, played three times for his country.

That side also did pretty well and they won the Test series, albeit by the narrowest of margins.

The tourists lost to Australia in the first international after stringing together three victories at the start of the tour. They also lost to Queensland and Metropolitan but won the remaining 18 games in a 21-match schedule.

The second and third Tests were won in convincing fashion but they barely scraped through in the final game to take the series 3-1.

1899 RESULTS

Played	Won	Drew	Lost	For	Against
21	18	0	3	333	90

Central Southern	W 11-3
New South Wales	W 4-3
Metropolitan	W 8-5
AUSTRALIA	L 3-13
Toowoomba	W 19-5
Queensland	L 3-11
Bundaberg	W 36-3
Rockhampton	W 16-3
Mount Morgan	W 29-3
Central Queensland	W 22-3
Maryborough	W 27-8
AUSTRALIA	W 11-0
New England	W 6-4
Northern	W 28-0
New South Wales	W 11-5
Metropolitan	L 5-8
Western	W 19-0
AUSTRALIA	W 13-0
Schools	W 21-3
Victoria	W 30-0
AUSTRALIA	W 11-10

1903: SOUTH AFRICA

I.G. Davidson (NIFC) and Hugh Ferris (Queen's University, Belfast) played together for Ireland three times - against Scotland and Wales in 1900 and against Wales in 1901.

How ironic it would have been then, had these two fellow-countrymen been drawn in opposition when yet another British/Irish team travelled to South Africa in 1903.

Ferris, who had played altogether four times for Ireland, was set to line out for his adopted country, South Africa, to which he had emigrated the previous year.

The confrontation was not to be, for while Davidson played in the first test match that ended in a 10-10 draw, he failed to win a place in the remaining two internationals.

The second international was also drawn (0-0) and Ferris, by all accounts, made a handsome contribution for the home side in the third game on a September day in 1903, helping them to an 8-0 victory and to the series.

Davidson was one of five Irishmen on that particular tour and the only back, but while this was the worst trip by a British side up to then, the Irish were certainly not to blame.

They provided four of the 11 forwards, and each of them - A. D. Tedford (Malone), R. S. Smyth (Dublin University) and brothers Joseph and James Wallace (Wanderers) – did well.

It was perhaps time that Ireland should produce another for-ward in the mould of Tommy Crean, and they did, in Tedford.

He was highly regarded by the South Africans and assessed as a marvellous scrummager and runner. Small in stature, he made up for that with pace, stamina and anticipation. A most durable player, he played in all three Tests and eventually won 23 caps for Ireland.

James Wallace was uncapped when embarking on the trip, but he made such an impression that he played in two of the interna-tionals and then returned home to win two Irish caps in 1904. His brother, Joseph, had an international career spanning four seasons and won a total of ten caps, playing in one Test in South Africa. The fourth Irish forward was R. S. Smith, who played in all the Tests on tour and scored one try.

But even the best efforts of the Irish could not deny South Africa revenge this time. It was a very strong British and Irish side, but yet they lost the first three matches - all against different Western Province teams. They had a run of five wins, and then lost three more in a row. Their last provincial defeat came against Transvaal. They drew the first two Tests but lost the series when they were defeated in the last in Cape Town.

1903 RESULTS

Played	Won	Drew	Lost	For	Against
22	11	3	8	229	138

Western Province (Country)	L 7-13
Western Province (Town)	L 3-12
Western Province	L 4-8
Port Elizabeth	W 13-0
Eastern Province	W 12-0
Grahamstown	W 28-7
King Williams Town	W 37-3
East London	W 7-5
Griqualand West	L 0-11
Griqualand West	L 6-8
Transvaal	L 3-12
Pretoria	W 15-3
Petermaritzburg	W 15-0
Durban	W 22-0
Witwatersrand	W 12-0
Transvaal	L 4-14
SOUTH AFRICA	D 10-10
Orange River Colony	W 17-16
Griqualand West	W 11-5
SOUTH AFRICA	D 0-0
Western Province	D 3-3
SOUTH AFRICA	L 0-8

Lions 1903 with Autographs

35

CHAPTER 4

A CAPTAIN AT LAST

Ireland's long wait for a leader of an overseas tour ended in 1910, when Dr Tom Smyth of Malone and Newport was given the honour of heading a party of 30 players on a 24-match trip to South Africa.

This was the first official representation of the four home unions and Smyth's fine performance for Ireland in the three preceding seasons suggested that he was the ideal man for the job. Certainly, all accounts of the tour confirm that he was an excellent leader, even if the results did not always favour his side.

In fact, they were rather inconsistent. While the party won 13 games, they lost another eight and drew three. South Africa won two of the three internationals, despite the best efforts of Smyth and the "man of the tour", young Englishman, "Cherry" Pillman. The latter started out as a wing-forward, but played in the second Test at out-half, helping his side to an eight points to three victory.

Smyth won a total of 14 caps for his country between 1908 and 1912 and was the most experienced Irishman on this tour.

But another Northern Ireland man, A. R. Foster of Derry, who had only just sprung to international prominence, was to emulate him, winning 17 caps altogether, the final one in 1921. Foster was one of six Irishmen in South Africa in 1910 and finished as second top try-scorer, after England's M. E. Neale.

Two more Northern Ireland players, W.Tyrrell, a student at Queens University, and A. N. Clinton (NIFC) accompanied Smyth and Foster.

Tyrrell had come into the Irish team before the touring party departed for South Africa and although he did not play in the test side, he had a good tour. He later went on to win 9 caps for his country.

McClinton had played against Wales and France that year but on tour did not play well enough to get in for the internationals.

The news that two Cork men - 0. J. S. Piper (Constitution) and W. J. Ashby (Queen's College Cork) - had been included was joyously welcomed in the Southern capital for they became the first players from the city to be so honoured. Ashby was uncapped at the time and did not make a great impression, but the established international, Piper, had a marvellous tour, playing in the first Test when the visiting side went down by 14 points to 10.

So, despite some poor results, history at least was made with the elevation of Tom Smyth to captain. And if the tour was, overall, a disappointing one, it set a precedent, for many more Irishmen were to be singled out for a similar honour.

The problems began after a five match unbeaten opening sequence. Griqualand West and Transvaal proved too strong for the visitors and so did Cape Colony.

After a warm-up victory over Rhodesia, they lost the first game to South Africa by 14-10. Although they hit back to take a win in the second game, they lost the third by the considerable margin, in those days, of 16 points.

1908: ANGLO-WELSH TOUR TO AUSTRALIA & NEW ZEALAND

Played	Won	Drew	Lost	For	Against
26	16	1	9	323	201

1910 RESULTS

Played	Won	Drew	Lost	For	Against
24	13	3	8	290	236

South-West Districts	W 14-4
Western Provinces (Country)	W 9-3
Western Provinces (College)	W 11-3
Western Provinces (Town)	D 11-11
Western Province	W 5-3
Griqualand West	L 0-8
Transvaal	L 8-27
Pretoria	W 17-0
Transvaal (Country)	W 45-4
Transvaal	L 6-13
Natal	W 18-16
Natal	W 19-13
Orange River Colony	W 12-9
Griqualand West	L 3-9
Cape Colony	L 0-19
Rhodesia	W 24-11
SOUTH AFRICA	L 10-14
North-East Districts	D 8-8
Border	W 30-10
Border	D 13-13
Eastern Province	W 14-6
SOUTH AFRICA	W 8-3
SOUTH AFRICA	L 5-21
Western Province	L 0-8

1924: SOUTH AFRICA

When Lansdowne and Irish half-back, W. Cunningham, left the shores of Ireland in 1923, bound for a new life in South Africa, little did he know that within months he would be joining forces with former colleagues against friends in his new homeland. Rather the opposite of the situation that faced Hugh Ferris 21 years earlier.

This British and Irish side, which at this time was generally referred to as "The Lions", had severe injury problems. It was so bad that, before the first test, one of the three quarters had to be drafted into the pack in order to make up the eight. The introduction of Cunningham, then, came directly as a result of injury to key players, but that is not to say that he did not contribute. He certainly did.

Capped by Ireland eight times between 1920 and 1923, Cunningham seemed set for a long international career before he decided to emigrate. While the Lions did not have a happy tour results-wise - they lost nine and drew three of their 21 games - Cunningham scored a magnificent try in the third test – the only one of the four games in which the tourists managed to avoid defeat. Cunningham, the reserve, was the only Irish back to have taken part, and it was a strange quirk of fate that he should have been responsible for their best international performance.

The 1924 pack was strong and tough, and played hard. It included a man who had only that season burst onto the Irish scene: J. M. McVicker of Collegians, who appeared in three of the tests and then went on to a most distinguished career in the Irish jersey, winning a total of 20 caps by 1930.

Another on board was Jammie Clinch (Dublin University and Wanderers), whose fame spread throughout the rugby world within a short time of his return from South Africa. When he travelled on that tour, he had not really established himself on the Irish side, although he had won five caps. He did not make the Test teams but returned home having obviously learned a great deal from his

39

experience, for he enjoyed a further seven seasons representing Ireland and finally won 30 caps.

Clinch was as colourful a character as any of the greats who went before him. A man who liked individuality, he was still a dedicated team player and was one of the tough-est men ever to don the Irish jersey.

He apparently got his nickname, Jammie, because he was said to have devoted a lot of time to making jam sandwiches in school, when his attentions might better have been given to books. That name was to follow him through life and, indeed, up to his death a couple of decades ago, he was well known for his appearances on RTE sports programmes, when he analysed the Irish rugby teams and the problems they were facing then.

At times, it seemed, he was less than kind to some players of the present day, but he was always a man to speak his mind.

T. N. Brand (NIFC) was uncapped when selected for the tour and although on his return he played once for Ireland, when they lost 6-0 to New Zealand, he never played at that level again. However, he did well in South Africa in 1924, so well, in fact, that he was included in two of the Tests and, according to the records available, his overall contribution was a handsome one.

Dolphin's M. J. Bradley was a famous Irish forward of the 1920s and in both 1926 and 1927 he helped Ireland to a share in the International championship with Scotland.

In all he was capped 19 times. He did not play in the Tests but he was reckoned to be a good Lions tourist.

Newport created something of a record in the 1910 tour, when they had more representatives than any other club. They contin-ued that trend in 1924 by having four of their men included. One of these was Dr W. J. Roche, who had won three caps for Ireland in 1920. Roche was from Cork and had played the first time for his country while he was a student at University College, Cork.

This was undoubtedly a good year for the Springboks who won the Test series with something to spare. It was tough enough going in the first but they wrapped up the series with a convincing win in the second game and a draw in the third. The Lions, licking their wounds, were in no form for more battle in the last Test of the tour and the only consolation was a late victory they scored in the final match against Western Province.

1924 RESULTS

Played	Won	Drew	Lost	For	Against
21	9	3	9	175	155

Western Province (Town and Country)	L	6-7
Western Province (Universities)	W	9-8
Griqualand West	W	26-0
Rhodesia	W	16-3
Western Transvaal	W	8-7
Transvaal	D	12-12
Orange Free State (Country)	L	0-6
Orange Free State	L	3-6
Natal	D	3-3
SOUTH AFRICA	L	3-7
Witwatersrand	L	6-10
SOUTH AFRICA	L	0-17
Pretoria	L	0-6
Cape Colony	W	13-3
North-East Districts	W	20-12
Border	W	12-3
Eastern Province	L	6-14
SOUTH AFRICA	D	3-3
South-West Districts	W	12-6
SOUTH AFRICA	L	9-16
Western Province	W	8-6

1930: NEW ZEALAND AND AUSTRALIA

More than 20 years after the Anglo-Welsh tour to New Zealand, the 1930 British Isles side set out for further combat with the All Blacks. It was a trip that took them not just to New Zealand, but also to Australia, and they finished with a tour record of 20 wins and eight losses.

Crucially, four of those defeats came in Test games. After winning the first against the All Blacks, the Lions then capitulated on three successive occasions to New Zealand and also lost to Australia when they travelled across the Tasman.

It might well have become known as the "Baggy Pants" tour, for the visitors were clad in rather clumsy-looking shorts, sporting large pockets to keep their hands warm during periods of inactivity (if any).

Yet while they lost the test series 1-3 in New Zealand, having had that encouraging start, it was otherwise a fairly successful undertaking, and their points tally of 624 was the biggest by any touring side up to then.

In keeping with the new tradition, there was a fair sprinkling of Irish blood in the party.

Five players in all from Ireland made the trip: P. F. Murray (Wanderers), the only back, G. R. (George) Beamish (Leicester), M. J. Dunne (Lansdowne), J. L. Farrell (Bective) and H. O'H. O'Neill (Queen's University).

Beamish was the most experienced of the Irish players and was regarded as one of the best foreign forwards ever seen in New Zealand. Naturally enough then, with several Irish caps behind him and more to come (25 in all), he played a major role in making the tour, despite the Test disappointments, a reasonably good one, particularly from the scoring point of view. He played in all the Tests.

J. L. Farrell was another of the stalwarts. He played 29 times altogether for Ireland, first in 1926, and like Beamish, he appeared in all of the Tests. So too did H. O'H. O'Neill, who sprang to prominence with Queen's University, but who later moved to University College, Cork, to further his studies.

P. F. Murray of Wanderers played in three Tests in New Zealand and the one in Australia.

1930 RESULTS

Played	Won	Drew	Lost	For	Against
28	20	0	8	624	318

Wanganui	W	19-3
Taranaki	W	23-7
Manawhenua	W	34-8
Wairarapa & Bush	W	19-6
Wellington	L	8-12
Canterbury	L	8-14
Buller/West Coast	W	34-11
Otago	W	33-9
NEW ZEALAND	W	6-3
Southland	W	9-3
Ashburton/South Canterbury/North Otago		
	W	16-9
NEW ZEALAND	L	10-13
Maoris	W	19-13
Hawkes Bay	W	14-3
East Coast/Poverty Bay/Bay of Plenty	W	25-11
Auckland	L	6-19
NEW ZEALAND	L	10-15
North Auckland	W	38-5
Waikato/Thames Valley/King Country	W	40-16
NEW ZEALAND	L	8-22
Marlborough/Nelson & Golden Bay	W	41-3
New South Wales	W	29-10
AUSTRALIA	L	5-6
Queensland	W	26-16
Australian XV	W	29-14
New South Wales	L	3-28
Victoria	W	41-36
Western Australia (unofficial)	W	71-3

Ireland V. France 1910

Back Row: O. Piper (5th), Middle Row: A. R. Foster (1st), A. McClinton (2nd), In front: W. Tyrrell (1st), All 1910 Lions.

46

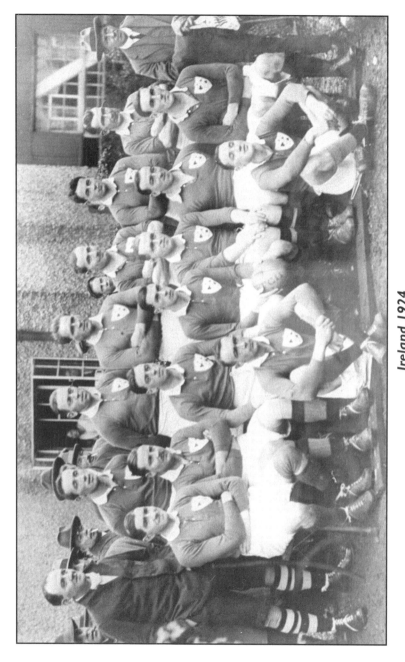

Ireland 1924

J. McVicker, J. Clinch and T. Brand included in this Irish team, went to South Africa later that year.

1930 Lions Included are G. Beamish, P. Murray, M. Dunne, J. Farrell and H O'H. O'Neill

48

CHAPTER 5

FOUR IN A ROW

Belfast prop forward, Sammy Walker, became the second Irish captain of the Lions when he led a party of 29 players, eight of them Irish, to South Africa in 1938.

It might never have happened, for Walker, while playing rugby in school, was said to have preferred Association Football, often incurring the wrath of games masters for pursuing his interest in that code.

Later in his life, however, it became quite apparent that his future lay in rugby. He was tough, he was strong, and his reputation as a superb scrummager helped win him a place on the Irish team in 1934, after a few seasons of great displays for his club, Instonians, and for his province, Ulster.

The 1938 Lions will not be remembered for a series win, because quite simply they failed. But they will never be forgotten for an unlikely, quite sensational, victory in the final test that saved a "whitewash". Sammy Walker and the remainder of the Irish contingent all took part in that famous victory. The fact that eight Irishmen were on that side is unique. It never happened before, and the chances of it happening again are remote.

It should be pointed out that this squad was riddled with injury in South Africa, which probably accounted for the large Irish representation in the final test. Nevertheless, the inclusion of so many Irish players was to prove highly rewarding.

The Lions had been beaten fairly badly in the two preceding internationals by a Danie Craven-inspired South African side, the bulk of whom had undertaken a successful tour to Australia and New Zealand some months before. In those first Tests the South Africans scored 45 points to the Lions' combined total of 15. They had scored seven tries as against one by the Lions.

It seemed as though the scene was set for a dismal end for Sammy Walker and his party. The signs looked even more ominous at half time, when the Lions trailed by ten points on a 13-3 score line.

But Walker had other ideas; within two minutes of the resumption of play, he inspired the comeback, sending in Englishman G. T. Dancer for the try after a fine break. Harry McKibbin added the points and then kicked a penalty to put them within sight of victory, before another Irish-man, Bob Alexander, gave them the lead with a great try, set up for him by George Cromey (Queen's University).

The Springboks went back in front with a penalty but Scottish full-back G. F. Grieve, deputising for the injured Vivian Jenkins (Wales), dropped a goal - worth four points - and his compatriot, P. L. Duff, sealed it with a try before the end: 21-16 to the Lions!

Thus Sammy Walker finished a happy international career on a winning note. He had played for Ireland on 15 occasions, but did not reappear for the one season left before the outbreak of World War II.

C. R. A. Graves of Wanderers, who played in two of those tests, had a career remarkably similar to that of Walker, winning 15 caps beginning and ending in the same seasons as his colleague.

The remainder of the Irish contingent went on to appear for their country in 1939. C. V. Boyle (Dublin University), who also had two test appearances in South Africa, won a total of nine caps, the last against Wales in the following season.

Harry McKibbin (Queen's University) had only one cap to his credit en route to the Southern hemisphere, but after three test outings and having scored 30 points on tour, he won three more caps for his country.

Undoubtedly the real character of the side was Queen's University player Blair Mayne, who was one of the four Irishmen to have appeared in all three tests. Mayne was a tough forward in the mould of Tommy Crean, and he became yet another to distinguish himself in wartime, making his name in the Middle East with the Special Air Service. In all, Mayne played six times for his country between 1937 and 1939.

Bob Alexander of NIFC was equally effective on the tour, scoring six tries, none more important than the crucial one in the third test. He won his first cap in 1936 and was a regular until 1939, appearing 11 times altogether.

The halfbacks for that final test were George Cromey, the fifth of the Ulster men in the party, and C. J. Morgan (Clontarf). For both, it was their only appearance against the Springboks, and how well they took their chance!

They combined magnificently together, and, like the rest of the side, covered themselves in glory. Cromey had come onto the Irish team in 1937 and played nine times between then and 1939. Morgan was there longer, having worked his way on back in 1934, and he won a total of 19 caps, the last in 1939.

1938 RESULTS

Played	Won	Drew	Lost	For	Against
23	17	0	6	407	272

Border	W	11-8
Griqualand West	W	22-9
Western Province (Town & Country)	L	8-11
South-West Districts	W	19-10
Western Province	L	11-21
Western Transvaal	W	26-9
Orange Free State	W	21-6
Orange Free State (Country)	W	18-3
Transvaal	L	9-16
Northern Transvaal	W	20-12
Cape Province	W	10-3
Rhodesia	W	25-11
Rhodesia	W	45-11
Transvaal	W	17-9
SOUTH AFRICA	L	12-26
Northern Province	L	8-26
Natal	W	15-11
Border	W	19-11
North-East District	W	42-3
Eastern Province	W	6-5
SOUTHAFRICA	L	3-19
SOUTH AFRICA	W	21-16
Combined University	W	19-16
Western Province Country (unofficial)	L	7-12

1950: NEW ZEALAND AND AUSTRALIA

When Karl Mullen was appointed captain of the Lions for their 1950 tour to New Zealand and Australia, it was another "first" in the history of the team's activities.

He was the first South of Ireland Catholic to lead representatives from Britain and Ireland overseas. The selectors seemed to have little doubt that Mullen, who led Ireland to Grand Slam and Triple Crown victories, would be the ideal captain, but they were still apprehensive. So much so that he was summoned to London.

Mullen recalls: "I think people were scared that I might have been a Fenian. I assured them of course that I was not, and promised there would be no politics."

It had been 20 years since the last Lions tour to those countries and, on the playing front; he was given the instruction to have his team run the ball at every opportunity. It was to be a "goodwill" tour, during which the Lions would show the very best of what British and Irish rugby had to offer and New Zealand would do the same.

Certainly New Zealand went through their paces, play-ing so well that they won the Test series without the loss of a single match. The Lions drew the first game but lost the next three.

In a sense, New Zealand broke their side of the bargain, for while Mullen's Lions were showing gay abandon in the use of their backs, the All Blacks were playing it tight, determined to win at all costs.

The shrewd use of a powerful pack, allied to a mundane but efficient back division, gave them the series.

Mullen admits: "If I had my way, we might have played differently. Certainly we had many great backs and it would have been foolish not to use players like Jack Kyle, Bleddyn Williams, Jack Matthews and Ken Jones, but I was used to Irish rugby and that meant playing it tight. Here we were committed to the type of stuff that the Barbarians produce. It was very popular but I feel it cost us the series, or at least a share of the spoils."

However Mullen, who went on to become an eminent Dublin gynaecologist, was happy that Ireland's contribution to the Lions was recognised fully for the first time in 1950, when a new strip of red shirts, white shorts and blue stockings with a green fringe was devised.

He may not have been satisfied with the test results but was extremely pleased with the Irish performances on tour. And Mullen was quite emphatic when he declared: "There would have been no tour without Jack Kyle".

His admiration for Ireland's legendary out-half, who was in "full flight" on this tour, was clear.

Kyle teased and tantalised both Australia and New Zealand with a series of brilliant displays, all of which prompted even the most partisan of fans to declare he was the best they had ever seen. That opinion has been endorsed many times over. Kyle played in all the tests, and if he was only seventh in the list of top try-scorers with a total of seven, he contributed to many more. He graced the Irish jersey on 46 occasions altogether - a record for a fly half - and his international career spanned 12 seasons.

Kyle was one of three Queen's University players on the tour; the other two were Noel Henderson and Bill McKay.

Henderson, at 21 years of age, had three internationals behind him and because of that lack of experience was not expected to challenge Williams and Matthews in the centre. In the event, he could not break up the partnership, but his form was so good that he played in one Test against the All Blacks - on the wing. He scored eight tries on tour and went on to a great career with Ireland, winning 40 caps by 1959 before later becoming a top official of the Irish Rugby Football Union.

Apart from the captain, Mullen, and Kyle, perhaps the biggest Irish influence on the tour was flanker Bill McKay who played in all six Tests. McKay is reckoned by many to have been the greatest

Irish flanker of all time and his displays in New Zealand in particular won him great praise. "His contribution was enormous. His fitness, determination and work rate was a spur to all of us", said Mullen, who recalled that having broken his nose, McKay was fitted with a special harness to protect his face, and he then lined out the following week in one of the Test games.

McKay was another Irishman who distinguished himself in battle. During World War Two he joined the British Army and was one of the famous "Wingate Raiders" Commando unit. He was twice sent on missions behind Japanese lines in Burma, and on one occasion was one of only a few dozen who returned.

Bill McKay enjoyed the tour to New Zealand, which established him as one of the great rugby characters. During that time he was studying medicine and before departing, he entrusted a medical book to the care of legendary Limerick forward, Tom Clifford.

Several times during the tour Clifford proffered it, but each time McKay turned him down. He finally took back the book when the party arrived back in London, over six months later. That particular period of inactive study did not seem to hamper the wing-forward because he did qualify as a doctor.

Jim Nelson (Malone) was the last of the Northern Ireland contingent and his value as a tight forward, and a good ball handler and dribbler was displayed several times on tour. Nelson went on to become one of the top administrators in the game and in 1982 completed a year as President of the Irish Rugby Football Union.

On the 1950 tour he played in four Tests - two in New Zealand and two in Australia. A member of the triumphant Irish Triple Crown teams in 1948 and 1949, his international career began in 1947 and ended in 1954, during which period he won a total of 16 caps.

The tour ended almost before it began for Bective's George Norton who broke his arm early on... and thereby hangs a tale. There has always been a great deal of controversy about the New Zealand attitude to players lying on the ball. Unwittingly or otherwise, Norton "transgressed" and suffered the consequences - a broken arm -which brought to an end his influence on the playing side of the tour.

Mullen's reaction? "Their attitude was different to ours and I suppose in a way they had a point on the law. They made no apologies for the incident. In their view he should not have been there."

In any event, the incident seemed to have little effect on Norton's enjoyment of the tour off the pitch. He was, by all accounts, a witty and likeable character and one story from Mullen sums him up.

The captain was always conscious of the behaviour of his players. This, after all, was a goodwill tour, and as leader he was responsible for their actions off the park. On leaving one particular hotel after a four-day stay, he was approached by the manager. "Here goes," said Mullen to himself, "What have they done?"

Earlier in the week the players had been supplied with crates of Guinness and for some "unknown" reason the crates had also been packed with straw. Mullen was surprised by the mild behaviour of the manager, who proceeded to thank him profusely, but then the question was posed:

"Would you please tell me how did the horse get into room 406?" It transpired that George Norton was registered in that room, although, admitted Mullen, "one cannot say he was responsible!"

It was not quite a great tour as far as Jim McCarthy (Dolphin) was concerned. McCarthy had a brilliant career for Ireland, lasting from 1948 to 1955, but his style was not suited to New Zealand rugby and so, although acquitting himself excellently in several provincial games, he failed to make the Test series. He did, however, score four fine tries.

McCarthy's Cork colleague, Mick Lane of UCC, who was first capped in 1947, and who shared in the Triple Crown victory of 1949 with him, fared better. Lane played a Test match in each of the countries and scored a total of four tries on tour. By the end of his international career in 1953, he had won 17 caps for Ireland.

When Tom Clifford arrived home to Limerick after his lengthy trip, a crowd of almost 8,000 took to the streets to welcome him. Marching bands appeared on virtually every street corner and the Young Munster prop forward, who brought fame to his club and city, was feted lavishly. He deserved it, for after all he was the first member of a Shannonside club to be selected for the Lions.

Clifford had a brilliant tour, according to Mullen, and his performances in New Zealand and Australia are well documented. He played in five of the six Tests and if one outstanding forward had to be chosen, then Clifford strongly challenged McKay for that honour.

Off the pitch, Clifford was equally popular and many funny stories have been told about him. On one occasion he scared the life out of Mullen by saying he would refuse to stand for the British National Anthem. Another time, he marched behind a brass band in Nelson, insisting they had turned out only for him.

A genial character, Clifford, however, took some things seriously, and food was one of them. Renowned for his prowess at the dinner table, he went through the entire menu consisting of 18 courses one evening on board the liner "Ceramic" en-route to New Zealand. Not alone did he astound the team colleagues who said it could not be done, but he also won the bet!

1950 RESULTS

Played	Won	Drew	Lost	For	Against
29	22	1	6	570	174

Nelson/Marlborough/Golden Bay & Motueka	W	24-3
Buller	W	24-9
West Coast	W	32-3
Otago	L	9-23
Southland	L	0-11
NEW ZEALAND	D	9-9
South Canterbury	W	27-8
Canterbury	W	16-5
Ashburton County/North Otago	W	29-6
NEW ZEALAND	L	0-8
Wairarapa and Bush	W	27-3
Hawkes Bay	W	20-0
Poverty Bay/Bay of Plenty/East Coast	W	27-3
Wellington	W	12-6
NEW ZEALAND	L	3-6
Wanganui	W	21-3
Taranaki	W	25-3
Manawatu and Horowhenua	W	13-8
Waikato/Thames Valley/King Country	W	30-0
North Auckland	W	8-6
Auckland	W	32-9
NEW ZEALAND	L	8-11
New Zealand Maoris	W	14-9
New South Wales (Country)	W	47-3
New South Wales	W	22-6
AUSTRALIA	W	19-6
AUSTRALIA	W	24-3
Metropolitan Union	W	26-17
New South Wales XV	L	12-17
Ceylon (Unofficial)	W	44-6

1955: SOUTH AFRICA

Who was it coined the phrase that the All Blacks were "lucky to get nil" when beaten 12-0 by Munster at Thomond Park on October 31, 1978?

Well, whoever used it on that occasion actually stole the line from Tom Reid, the Garryowen and Irish forward.

Tony O'Reilly, who toured with Reid on the 1955 Lions tour to South Africa, tells the following story: "Having first seen Tom in action on tour when he was the cement and mortar of the side that pulled us all together, I didn't realise he was not noted for the avidity with which he trained. I'd last seen him in Pretoria as we boarded the plane to fly home and the following February we met again in London for the match against England.

I noted in the dressing room that Tom was extremely vigorous in the pre-match warm-up and I said: "For God's sake you'll exhaust yourself.

"His reply was, 'Jesus, Reilly, this is the first run I've had since Pretoria.' He went out and, like all of us, proceeded to prove it was the first run since Pretoria, for we were hammered 20-0. Coming off the pitch, pursued by every hospital orderly, fly-over constructor and trench-digger in the greater London area, I said to him, 'Wasn't that awful?' Back came the reply: 'Yes, Reilly, and weren't we lucky to get nil?'

O'Reilly has a very definite affection for Reid, respecting him far more than most of his colleagues on that tour and his subsequent tour to New Zealand in 1959.

He commented: "I should think the 1955 tour was the first time in his life that Reid was really fully fit and he played a major role in the success of the tour. We had won one and lost another of the first two tests and then we went 2-1 up in the series with a 9-6 win in the third game. In my opinion, Tom Reid effectively won that game for us because of his dominance at the back of the line-out. He proved more than once that he was something other than a quick tongue and a golden voice and was one of the major successes of the tour, doing superbly in the two tests in which he played."

Reid was one of five Irish players on that side which drew the series 2-2 with South Africa. A quick-witted fellow, he had sharp competition in that field from Cecil Pedlow, undoubtedly one of the most accomplished athletes ever to wear the Irish jersey. Pedlow was a Davis cup standard tennis player, a squash international and a superb footballer who could kick with either foot. On tour, Pedlow was a regular try-scorer and goal-kicker and ended up as top scorer with 58 points.

O'Reilly describes him: "In his own view, I think he believed he lacked pace for the wing, but he was an outstandingly good utility player and deservedly got in for two Tests.

"Off the field, he had a lightning Northern wit, captured by a story of a friend of mine who once came to stay with us. He was writing a book about Belfast and when I told Cecil about this and introduced them, he replied: 'he'd better be quick!'

"Pedlow had a great sense of fun. He had problems with his eyesight and he used to take off his glasses, always protesting to the girls that they should get closer to him so he could see them properly. But of course his eyesight also posed problems, especially under the high kick when he used to shout 'my ball' as it dropped 40 yards away! He was the perfect tourist and a man who could live with both victory or defeat at either personal or team level."

Robin Thompson (Instonians) captained that 1955 side, but unfortunately illness curtailed his contribu-tion to the tour. He did play in three of the tests, but in the final game, when he came back after an operation for the removal of his appendix, he was not the same force he had been before his illness.

Robin Roe was capped 21 times for Ireland between 1952 and 1957 and the Lansdowne hooker gave sterling service to his country during that time, easily earning his place on the 1955 Lions tour. Unfortunately he came up against daunting competition from Bryn Meredith, described by O'Reilly as one of the greatest hookers he had ever seen in action. Roe had unfortunately damaged his ribs very early on in the tour and that kept him out of action for some time. Yet he played very well once he had recovered and became one of the most popular members of the party.

Roe, who was a Protestant Clergyman, came in for some ribbing because of the enormity of his neck. The Catholics in the group used to tell him he had a great neck for a Roman Catholic collar. The Lansdowne man was noted for his achievements in areas other than rugby, winning the Military Cross in Aden while serving as Chaplain to the British forces.

"That did not surprise me. Robin Roe is a man with a strong sense of the heroic . . . a great man in many respects," says O'Reilly.

Fuzzy Anderson of Queen's University and NIFC was, according to O'Reilly, a world-class prop-forward. He had played 13 times for Ireland by the time he was selected for the Lions. Unfortunately illness struck and he had to withdraw from the tour.

O'Reilly remembers the Welsh game earlier that year: "I'll swear that Fuzzy was having a heart attack in the bath after that game. I looked at him and said, 'you look terrible.' Some time later he went into hospital for a full check-up and he had to undergo major heart surgery which obviously ended his rugby career prematurely."

All of these men, apart, of course, from Anderson, made a major contribution to that 1955 tour, and none did better than O'Reilly himself, who scored 16 tries. It was a huge achievement.

O'Reilly goes back over the story of his rapid rise to international rugby for Ireland and then selection on the Lions.

"I had the good fortune of getting into the Irish team when I was only eighteen and a half. I played only three senior club games before being named in the Leinster team to meet Ulster, but I decided not to play - discretion being the better part of valour, since the conditions were very bad. I went climbing the Sugar Loaf instead and I learned a great deal about Irish rugby by not doing so. A reporter at the match decided the centres had not done too well that day and proclaimed that by comparison I must be the best centre in the country. By not playing, I did my prospects no harm and after one more club game, was named in the final trial, with my sixth senior match coming in an international against France."

The young Old Belvedere player did very well in his first season, well enough to be included in the 1955 Lions party that he was to serve so well. He enjoyed that tour thoroughly, although he said that when scoring his 16th try in the last minute of the final test, he dislocated his right shoulder and confesses that this was a weak point there-after: "From the try-scoring point of view, I had a great tour, but I paid the price for it, for my shoulder problem was a recurring event and it troubled me greatly at times."

He singles out the Lions' back line as being almost completely responsible for his try-scoring spree: "I was at the end of a legendary division - Jeeps, Morgan, Butterfield and Davies. What a way for the ball to get out to you!

"By the time the opposition had matched the threat of any one of that four, you were one on one. Right throughout my international career I had to face more than one defender, and once I became well known, I don't think I ever went on the pitch without two or three guys determined to make a name for themselves by knocking me into the stand.

"In South Africa I was unknown, and that, for the first part of the tour at least, was a great advantage. With men like that inside me I got great scoring opportunities and scored ten tries in my first six games. Things got a little tougher after that; I only scored six in my last ten matches and I suppose the aphorisms, which Cliff Morgan used to use are true: 'The gaps get smaller when your name gets bigger' and 'to be as good as you were, you have to be twice as good as you were.'

O'Reilly went to great pains to highlight the witty side of such players as Reid and Pedlow, but his own sense of fun is well documented. Even as a youthful 19-year old, he had begun to make his mark off the field. The manager of that tour was Jack Siggins of Collegians.

O'Reilly says: "Jack was an excellent manager but he took himself a bit seriously early on . . . that is, until Pedlow and myself got working on him, using sketches to press home our points. Thankfully he had the good humour to realise what we were at and, as the tour progressed, he became much more flexible and was very much one of the boys."

1955: SOUTH AFRICA

Played	Won	Drew	Lost	For	Against
25	19	1	5	457	283

Western Transvaal	L	6-9
Griqualand West	W	24-14
Northern Universities	W	32-6
Orange Free State	W	31-3
South West Africa	W	9-0
Western Province	W	11-3
South Western Districts	W	22-3
Eastern Province	L	0-20
North-Eastern Districts	W	34-6
Transvaal	W	36-13
Rhodesia	W	27-14
Rhodesia	W	16-12
SOUTH AFRICA	W	23-22
Central Universities	W	21-14
Boland	W	11-0
Western Province Universities	W	20-17
SOUTH AFRICA	L	9-25
Eastern Transvaal	D	17-17
Northern Transvaal	W	14-11
SOUTH AFRICA	W	9-6
Natal	W	11-8
Junior Springboks	W	15-12
Border	L	12-14
SOUTH AFRICA	L	8-22
East African XV	W	39-12

1959:
AUSTRALIA, NEW ZEALAND AND CANADA

If motivation was needed during the next Lions tour, then Irishman Dave Hewitt was surely the one to provide it. Sweat dripping from his brows in the fourth Test against New Zealand in 1959, Tony O'Reilly wondered whether the Lions could hold out, even though they had scored three tries to two penalties by the All Blacks.

He describes the action of that game: "We had been beaten late in the first and second Tests, had lost the third comprehensively but led 9-6 going into the final few minutes of the last. We were well on top but strange refereeing decisions had conspired to give them penalty chances. As they attacked, I stood on the line; deep in thought and thinking what my opposite number would do if he got the ball.

"Suddenly Dave Hewitt moved out towards me and with the crowd going crazy for an All Black score, says in a Northern Ireland accent: 'Have you seen that cloud formation up there. Why that's a very interesting and beautiful sky. I'm going to take a picture of that when this game is over.'

"I said to myself, 'My God, here is a man who is committed passionately to the game of rugby football!'

Hewitt was, by all accounts, a straightforward man. He was the recipient of many presentations, being, as he was, one of the most popular players on tour. A typical reception might go like this - one of the rugby alickadoos would stand up and say: "We are pleased to have the Lions with us this evening, and particularly Dave Hewitt, because he is such a great player. We would like you, Dave, to have these six pieces of glass which we hope you will bring back to Ireland with you."

Hewitt's stock reply was to say: "That's very kind of you; I am very pleased and thank you very much. But six pieces would be no good. I'd really need more than that." It was a joke, of course, but

65

Andy Mulligan, who joined the tour as a substitute, maintained that when the party left New Zealand, a 10,000 ton freighter followed carrying all the "loot" Dave Hewitt had been presented with on tour.

As well as the droll side of Hewitt, there was, of course, a very sharp brain. His international career began in 1958 and effectively concluded in 1962, although he did make a comeback in 1965. His biggest problem was injury, as he was prone to hamstring damage.

But in the good times he was absolutely brilliant. O'Reilly recalls: "When Dave Hewitt was on his game, he was an unstoppable force. He was not always consistent, but for sheer brilliance he must rank as one of the best centres of all time. On that 1959 tour, myself, Niall Brophy and J. R. C. Young could, along with Dave; all do the 100 yards in less than 10 seconds. But Hewitt would leave us all for dead over 50 yards. Hewitt may only have come fourth in terms of try-scoring on that tour, but he was top points scorer, for in addition to grabbing 13 tries, he kicked 20 conversions, 10 penalties and dropped a goal to give himself a total of 112 points."

Hewitt was one of ten Irishmen involved in that tour, although in the case of two of them - Niall Brophy and Mick English - the contribution was small. Brophy, who won 20 caps between 1957 and 1967, damaged an ankle without ever touching the ball. It happened, in fact, just before the kick-off in his first match of the tour and he never recovered from the injury. English, one of the great-est tactical kickers of a ball in the post-war era, was plagued by stomach strain and played only a limited number of games. He became known as "jog only". Manager Alf Wilson used to ask him before training whether he would be able to participate and when his condition was most acute, English would reply: "Sorry Alf, jog only." The two players finally returned home when it became clear that they would be unable to continue but legend has it, and that legend has never been denied by either, that they took the scenic route home.

66

By the time they arrived back in Ireland, the rest of the Lions party had already been home a couple of weeks!

The 1959 side was captained by yet another Irishman, Ronnie Dawson, who, like Ciaran Fitzgerald 24 years later, was to go through some soul-searching as to whether he should select himself for the final Test side.

Again Bryn Meredith was in the party and posed an obvious threat. But when Dawson approached some of the players to ask their opinion, he was told that unless there was a very clear playing difference between himself and Meredith, he owed it to all of the players to keep himself in. He did, and they won that last match.

Dawson formed an all-Irish front row partnership with the redoubtable Syd Millar and Gordon Wood, two players of contrasting styles. Millar has been described as "a fattish centre three-quarter playing in the front row because of his ability to run, dummy sidestep, and pass without any difficulties whatever."

Wood was less spectacular, but solid to the core, very fit and very strong - pretty immovable, in fact - and both made quite an impression when they played together.

His son Keith was to emulate him by gaining selection on both the Lions tour to South Africa in 1997 and Australia earlier this year.

In the second row was Bill Mulcahy who despite his lack of height, was one of Ireland's most successful forwards, winning himself 35 caps. He was arguably too small to be a second row, but yet had a high rate of success as a player. Cecil Pedlow, when asked by Tony O'Reilly what the lineout calls were before one international, replied: "Ah, just throw to the hole in the middle. They are crouching in a private trench."

Mulcahy himself, when asked how he would like the ball, is said to have reacted by saying, "low and crooked".

Mulcahy also suffered his share of injuries in New Zealand, but he was, according to O'Reilly, "never less than good and sometimes was superb. He was one of the most courageous footballers I have ever played with."

The Bective Rangers man played in one test against Australia and one against New Zealand.

In 1955 the youngest member of the party was O'Reilly. That distinction fell to another Irishman four years later. He was Cork man Noel Murphy, who was later to devote himself to coaching and managerial tasks as well. Ronnie Dawson described him then as a player whose basic talent was considerable. "He was the one above any of the others seen to be under the high dropping ball, showing no fear whatever."

O'Reilly, in one of his many quicksilver comments, said of him: "All he wants to do is die for Ireland."

O'Reilly continued: "Noel Murphy decided he'd make his name by standing under the high ball. I can still hear the New Zealand skies split by his high-pitched cries - in a Cork accent of course - of 'my ball'. That only matched the shouts of 14 other guys shouting in unison 'your ball!'

"Noel played extremely well. He was a damn good flank forward, wasn't a player of blinding pace, nor one of great broken field capabilities, but he had tremendous intelligence and had an instinct to be at the right place at the right time. He was not the flash type, but he was fearless and was always there to tidy up things."

Murphy's fine efforts won him a test place against Australia, and against New Zealand on three occasions during that long tour.

On every tour there are comedians, and if the 1955 duo of Pedlow and O'Reilly had split up, Andy Mulligan was there in 1959 to join the centre-turned-winger, O'Reilly off the field. The two combined to amuse the team, as well as New Zealand rugby fans and radio listeners throughout the country.

Mulligan, of Wanderers and London Irish, very nearly failed to make it. He was not an original selection, although tipped to be included in the party. When Scotsman Stan Coughtrie made the side before him, it came as a bitter disappointment to Mulligan for he had played extremely well in the international championship that had just been completed.

In any event, Coughtrie, a tall player for the position, was injured and Mulligan was called upon as a replacement.

O'Reilly takes up the story: "The number one, Dickie Jeeps, had fathomless strength and absolute courage, but he was not a great runner with the ball. He had no break, was an adequate kicker and a short passer. With an out-half like Cliff Morgan, that would have been permissible, but with Bev Risman, in many ways as talented as Morgan but without the same speed, one needed a longer pass. Mulligan could out-pass Jeeps by a substantial margin.

"The big question was, however, whether Mulligan would stand up to the hard stuff with the All Blacks forwards coming through on him. He proved he was durable. Jeeps played in the first three tests but Andy, in fair competition, won his place for the last game, and I would say that the single most important determinant in making victory in that game possible was his play. It was his brilliant open side break, and a superb flying, diving reverse pass to Risman going down the blind side, with me having run into the centre to decoy the back row which led to the final try; and, of course, he also set me up for my 17th try to break Ken Jones's record. He broke quickly down the blind, drew my wing and left me with a 10-yard drive to the line.

"Mulligan's courage was beyond doubt even before that and after that game his jersey had to be cut off him; such was the extent of the injuries on his chest, ribs and stomach. He was bleeding quite heavily and his ribs were red raw for two weeks after. But he helped win the game for us."

Off the field, O'Reilly, the contributor of 22 tries on a tour that took in Canada in addition to Australia and New Zealand, was the perfect partner to Mulligan. Between them, they entertained the masses with their "goon show", easing the pressure when things got hot for the team. After several appearances on radio, the two actually took to the stage in the last week of the tour.

Having already cut a disc, Mulligan and O'Reilly felt they had had enough training, yet they still had to participate.

O'Reilly says: "We needed some escape, so we signed on as a comedy team at the 'Hi Diddle Griddle' in Auckland, where I played the piano and Andy played the guitar. All went well because nobody knew we were there, but on the morning of the final test, there was this photograph which appeared in the local papers. Management were appalled. They had thought we had been in bed every night at 9 o'clock with our Horlicks!"

An example of Mulligan's wit? Going for his first job he was asked as a final question: "What religion are you, by the way?"

"Well sir, what religion had you in mind?" he quipped.

Yes, those obviously were the days.

1959:
AUSTRALIA, NEW ZEALAND AND CANADA

Played	Won	Drew	Lost	For	Against
33	27	0	6	842	353

Victoria	W	53-18
New South Wales	L	14-18
Queensland	W	39-11
AUSTRALIA	W	17-6
New South Wales Country Districts	W	27-14
AUSTRALIA	W	24-3
Hawkes Bay	W	52-12
East Coast and Poverty Bay	W	23-14
Auckland	W	15-10
New Zealand Universities	W	25-13
Otago	L	8-26
South Canterbury/North Otago/ Mid Canterbury	W	21-11
Southland	W	11-6
NEW ZEALAND	L	17-18
West Coast - Buller	W	58-3
Canterbury	L	14-20
Marlborough/Nelson/Golden Bay/Motueka	W	64-5
Wellington	W	21-6
Wanganui	W	9-6
Taranaki	W	15-3
Manawatu & Horowhenua	W	26-6
NEW ZEALAND	L	8-11
King Country and Counties	W	25-5
Waikato	W	14-0
Wairarapa and Bush	W	37-11
NEWZEALAND	L	8-22
New Zealand Juniors	W	29-9
New Zealand Maoris	W	12-6
Thames Valley and Bay of Plenty	W	26-24

North Auckland	W	35-13
NEW ZEALAND	W	9-6
British Columbia	W	16-11
Eastern Canada	W	70-6

Harry McKibben relaxes at Kroonstaad Bowling Green, South Africa, in 1938.

The Irish contingent on the 1938 tour take time out for a photo call.

Ireland V. Wales 1949 Back Row M. Lane (2nd), T. Clifford (3rd), J. Nelson (7th), G. Norton (8th), B. McKay 9th, Middle Row: J. McCarthy (1st) K. Mullen (3rd), N. Henderson (6th), J.W. Kyle (1st on ground). All Irish Lions.

The legendary Jackie Kyle and Tom Clifford await the outcome of this tussle in 1950.

One of the greatest exponents of the dribble, Tom Clifford, shows the way to captain Karl Mullen against Otago.

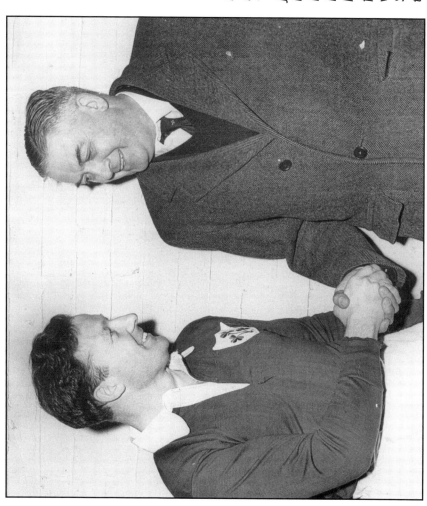

Rugby England v. Ireland, at Twickenham

Jackie Kyle (left) playing his 45th game for Ireland against against England in 1958, a home countries record for caps; shakes hands with Dr. G.V. Stephanson, prior to the match.

B. G. M. Wood holds a trout at Greenmeadows. M. A. English is on the left

A.J. F. O'Reilly

78

Bill Mulcahy and Ronnie Dawson in action

Andy Mulligan

79

No try this time for 1959 top scorer in New Zealand, tony O'Reilly, as Bill Mulcahy watches him drive over the touchline.

Captain for the day, Andy Mulligan introduces Lord Wakefield to Noel Murphy and the rest of the team.

1959 Lions 1st Row Back: D. Hewitt (1st), G. Wood 6th, A. Mulligan (4th), 2nd Row: S. Millar (1st), N. Brophy (3rd), 3rd Row: W. Mulcahy (1st), A. O'Reilly (6th), N., Murphy 8th, 4th Row: T. R. Dawson (Capt.) (4th), 5th Row: M. English (5th).

81

CHAPTER 6

THE SIXTIES

Four of the seven Irishmen included in the tour party for South Africa in 1962 were already experienced Lions and two of the others were, later on in their career, to become household names in world rugby.

1962: SOUTH AFRICA

Arthur Smith's 1962 side may have lost the test series, but there was a fair element of bad luck involved, for having drawn the opening international, they lost the second game 3-0, and the third 8-3. These were results that could easily have gone the other way.

The last Test result was embarrassing when South Africa rattled up a big total and won the game 34-14. It was an unusually high score for a Test match at the time.

Tom Kiernan, who with Englishman John Willcox was a fullback on the tour, recalls that the Lions should have won the second match. They forced a scrum near the Springboks' line and Bill Mulcahy, who was pack leader, called for a wheel. The pack drove over the home line and Keith Rowlands of Wales got the touchdown.

The South African referee refused to award the score, however, on the basis that he had been not seen anyone touch the ball down.

Most Lions' sides have had problems with referees on overseas trips and the 1962 tour was no exception.

Kiernan explained: "Rumour had it that the try was disallowed because the referee did not know which of the Lions got the try!"

South Africa had been leading 3-0 at the time and quickly after Rowland's claims for a score, the final whistle went, even though the visitors had just been awarded a scrum five yards out.

Kiernan did not play in the first or second internationals, a combination of ankle injuries and fine performances by Willcox damaging his progress, but he was included in the third test - one that the Lions might also have won. Included too that afternoon was Willie John McBride, who, like Kiernan, went on to become one of the best-known figures in the Irish game.

The former fullback and Irish coach had a great game that day, catching and kicking superbly and almost forging a try for Dickie Jeeps only seconds from the end. The Lions lost 3-8 but they might well have drawn, thus keeping the series on a "tightrope". With only a few minutes to go, they were level 3-3. In a desperate bid to win the match, they ran the ball from their own line and when a Richard Sharp pass went astray, Springbok player Keith Oxlee nipped in for the try that he converted himself.

It was a sad occasion for Kiernan and for three other Irish players - Willie John McBride, Sid Millar and Bill Mulcahy, who were in the side that day, but although the test series was lost, the entire Irish contingent earned praise for their performances throughout the trip.

McBride was the "baby" of the Lions pack at 21 years of age. He had only that season come onto the international team. He could hardly have expected to make the Test side, but although excluded for the first two, he was named for the others. His selection came as a shock to some, to Keith Rowlands in particular, who made way for him in the third Test.

But consultations with the record books and with those involved in the tour suggest clearly that McBride's rise to prominence was completely justified. He had shown steady improvement as the tour progressed, and in the 18th match against Transvaal - the last before the third Test – produced a brilliant display of jumping in the lineouts. His rucking and capable scrummaging also helped win him the Test place.

Haunted by an injury sustained three years before, Niall Brophy again had some problems in South Africa. Named in the side for the first Test, he damaged a shoulder during the match, and although he played on, it clearly limited his participation for the remainder of the tour.

He did come back to form to win a place against South Africa in the fourth match, but in all only played in five provincial matches, although he did score two fine tries. Brophy went on to win seven more caps for Ireland, two the following season, and then, after a period in the wilderness, five more in 1967, bringing his total to 20.

Bill Mulcahy was another player who had been to Australia, New Zealand and Canada in 1959, and this time around he was, with Syd Millar, the only Irishman to appear in all four Tests.

Mulcahy won himself a large fan club in 1962. He led a big pack into battle with the Springboks and much of the credit for their success up front has been attributed to him. Long before the end of the tour, the pack was being referred to as Mulcahy's "Boyos".

Mulcahy had, after his student days in UCD, moved on to Bohemians in Limerick, and he was the second player from that club to be honoured with selection for the Lions - the first being Mick English who had joined him three years before.

But while he and Brophy (Blackrock) had left college, two more Irishmen were still involved in Universities rugby. Kiernan, of course, was still with UCC while Dave Hewitt, another veteran from 1959, was attending Queen's University.

It was not a happy tour for Hewitt, because he suffered greatly from injuries. He played in seven matches, whereas, if fit, he would surely have participated in many more. He did score two tries and played in the last Test, but as far as his Irish International career was concerned, he was almost finished. His last appearance for Ireland came in 1965 against Wales, after two full seasons of International activity.

Ray Hunter of CIYMS failed to make the test teams, but scored two tries in 11 matches. Used as a utility back, he won a fair amount of praise at the time for his perform-ances, and he was looked upon as an excellent defender. Hunter won a total of 10 caps for his country.

Millar, of Ballymena, went on to become one of the greatest Irish forwards of all time. A superb prop-forward, he was also a shrewd tactician and he gave pack leader Mulcahy incredible support. He played 16 matches in all; only Mike Campbell Lamberton, Keith Rowlands and Mulcahy played more than him. He won 37 caps for Ireland, his career extending from 1958 to 1970, and after that rugby still played a major role in his life, for follow-ing three Lions tours as a player, he went on to coach the brilliant 1974 team in South Africa. Six years later he managed Billy Beaumont's Lions and then progressed to senior positions in the Irish Rugby Football Union, the Four Nations Committee and the International Board.

1962 RESULTS

Played	Won	Drew	Lost	For	Against
25	16	4	5	401	208

Rhodesia	W	38-9
Griqualand West	D	8-8
Western Transvaal	W	11-6
Southern Universities	W	14-11
Boland	W	25-8
South-West Africa	W	14-6
Northern Transvaal	L	6-14
SOUTH AFRICA	D	3-3
Natal	W	13-3
Eastern Province	W	21-6
Orange Free State	D	14-14
Junior Springboks	W	16-11
Combined Services	W	20-6
Western Province	W	21-13
South-Western Districts	W	11-3
SOUTH AFRICA	L	0-3
Northern Universities	D	6-6
Transvaal	W	24-3
SOUTH AFRICA	L	3-8
North-Eastern Districts	W	34-8
Border	W	5-0
Central Universities	W	14-6
Eastern Transvaal	L	16-19
SOUTH AFRICA	L	14-34
East Africa	W	50-0

1966:
AUSTRALIA, NEW ZEALAND AND CANADA

Michael Cameron Gibson's international career began in 1964 and finished, 69 international appearances later, in 1979. With 12 caps for the British and Irish Lions, he was for many years the most capped player in the world.

That record is now long since gone because countries throughout the rugby world are playing many more games each season than in Gibson's day.

By 1966, Gibson had won three Cambridge Blues and played for Ireland 13 times, but contrary to popular theory, it was not "unlucky 13".

The Irish out-half, later centre and even winger, made a dramatic impact on Mike Campbell Lamberton's Lions party to the three countries.

This was a tour steeped in controversy. For a start, Campbell Lamberton was a surprise choice as captain, despite the fact that he had been a successful tourist to South Africa four years earlier.

As events transpired, the big Scotsman stood down from some of the more important provincial matches. While he led the Lions to a series win in Australia and prompted them to their biggest ever win over that country in an International, Welshman Alun Pask, the vice-captain, would have been most people's choice for the captaincy.

However, despite Pask's influence, Mike Gibson, one of eight Irishmen in the party, was the star of the show.

In real terms, while Campbell Lamberton's Lions became the first overseas party to lose all matches in a series in New Zealand, they did not return with the worst record from that country.

What was true is that they found the going much tougher than at the start of the tour that began in Perth, Western Australia and continued through South Australia, New South Wales and

Queensland. The Lions played eight games in that sector of the tour and had seven wins and a draw.

In those times, Australia were clearly not up to the mark, although they did give the visitors a run for their money in the first Test before capitulating in the second.

The Lions weren't long learning that New Zealand would be a different challenge completely. They lost three of their six provincial matches, they put a better run together before the first Test but it didn't matter when the All Black heavyweights were produced.

But back to the Irish link . . . and to Gibson, who was treated as star of the side wherever he went. Welshman David Watkins was the senior fly half, playing in that position in all of the Tests in both Australia and New Zealand.

Gibson blazed such a trail in provincial games that he just had to be included eventually. He was picked in the centre for the first Test and partnered D. K. Jones of Cardiff and Wales.

Englishman Colin McFadyean, often the scourge of Ireland, was moved from the wing to centre and he partnered Gibson for the remaining three Tests. Both men performed with distinction, even if they failed to stop New Zealand from battling on to the first ever series "white-wash".

Gibson was one of nine Irishmen in the party. Only eight were originally selected, but Barry Bresnihan of UCD was flown in as a replacement. Although he was confined to appearances in provincial games, Bresnihan, 25 times capped for Ireland, scored five tries.

As a youngster, Jerry Walsh was tipped for the top. Those who thought him good enough to make the grade at international level were right. From his early days at Presentation Brothers' College, Cork, he starred in numerous schools sides. He won virtually every honour in the game including 21 caps for Ireland, until the final accolade, that of Lions selection, came.

Hopes were high that he would figure in the selectors' plans for the Test games. Sadly that dream did not materialise because he was forced to return home when his father died during the tour.

The fourth Irish back was Roger Young, the Queen's University scrumhalf, who won nine caps before the squad was announced.

Young eventually played for his country 26 times, before emigrating to South Africa. Young started out as number one scrum half but, after two Test appearances in Australia and one in New Zealand, he lost his place. So from his point of view, despite some great provincial performances, the tour ended in disappointment.

Ronnie Lamont failed to make the Test sides in Australia, but a series of brilliant performances in New Zealand won him a place on the side and he never lost it after that. Lamont had a chequered career with Ireland, winning seven caps in 1965 and 1966, and then losing his place before returning for the entire 1970 season.

Noel Murphy had, as a youngster, been on the 1959 tour to the same three countries. This time he was older and wiser, but still only managed to play in the same number of Tests as he did seven years before. There was a difference, for having played once against Australia and three times against the All Blacks on the previous tour, this time it was two and two.

He joined Barry Bresnihan, Mike Gibson, Ken Kennedy, Ray McLoughlin and Willie John McBride for the final international against Canada on the way home - a match which the Lions won by 19 points to eight and one in which Murphy scored two magnificent tries. He also scored in the second of the Australian Tests and had an overall total of six tries.

Willie John McBride was on his second tour, but his first trip to Australia and New Zealand. As on the 1962 South Africa tour, he was a marvellous success. Like Lamont and Murphy, he was one of the outstanding loose forwards.

No wonder then that he went on to become such a great personality in the game in later years. His attitude was that everyone should give 100 per cent all of the time and there were many at the time that tipped him for greater honours. Eight years later, they were all proved right.

Ken Kennedy was Ireland's most capped hooker. He played two Tests in both Australia and New Zealand and proved him-self extremely vigorous on the pitch and popular off it.

With Queens, CIYMS, and later with London Irish, Kennedy won a total of 45 Irish caps and he was selected to travel with McBride's all-conquering 1974 side to South Africa.

Ray McLoughlin, then of Gosforth, of Blackrock, Connacht and Ireland, was arguably one of the foremost tacticians in the early 1960s. He was included in the 1966 Lions party and enjoyed considerable success. He appeared in the two internationals in Australia and one in New Zealand, winning his place against stern opposition. He also returned to play in the international against Canada. McLoughlin lined out 40 times for Ireland, winning his first cap in 1962 and his last in 1975. In between he had a remark-able career and he is remembered as one of the best-known per-sonalities of the game.

The manager of the party was also an Irishman. Des O'Brien was extremely well liked by the public and the media but unfor-tunately suffered because of a string of bad results. While accept-ed as a genuine effort-seeker, the general consensus of opinion was that he did not instil enough discipline in the players when neces-sary.

1966 RESULTS

Played	Won	Drew	Lost	For	Against
35	23	3	9	524	345

Western Australia	W	60-3
South Australia	W	38-11
Victoria	W	24-14
Combined Country XV	W	6-3
New South Wales	D	6-6
AUSTRALIA	W	11-8
Queensland	W	26-3
AUSTRALIA	W	31-0
Southland	L	8-14
South Canterbury/North Otago		
Mid Canterbury	W	20-12
Otago	L	9-17
New Zealand Universities	W	24-11
Wellington	L	6-20
Nelson/Marlborough/Golden Bay		
Motueka	W	22-14
Taranaki	W	12-9
Bay of Plenty	D	6-6
North Auckland	W	6-3
NEW ZEALAND	L	3-20
West Coast/Buller	W	25-6
Canterbury	W	8-6
Manawatu/Horowhenua	W	17-8
Auckland	W	12-6
Wairarapa Bush	W	9-6
NEW ZEALAND	L	12-16
WanganuilKings Country	L	6-12

New Zealand Maoris	W	16-14
Poverty Bay/East Coast	W	9-6
Hawkes Bay	D	11-11
NEW ZEALAND	L	6-19
New Zealand Juniors	W	9-3
Waikato	W	20-9
Thames Valley/Counties	W	13-9
NEW ZEALAND	L	11-24
British Columbia	L	3-8
CANADA	W	19-8

1968: SOUTH AFRICA

In every British and Irish Lion there is a determination to do well in the Test series. After all, that is the primary aim. This was the case way back in 1888; it was the case 80 years later when Tom Kiernan became the sixth man from Ireland to lead the Lions.

Kiernan's job was a daunting one. Some of the players had been on Mike Campbell Lamberton's team two years before, and while it may be unjust to describe that as a disaster, it would be true to say that team spirit was not exactly at an all-time high.

Kiernan's brief was to deliver better results and also to ensure that this tour would be a happy one; that morale would be maintained throughout.

As far as results were concerned, he succeeded only to a point. South Africa won the series 3-O, with one game drawn, and from that viewpoint the 1968 Lions failed in their mission. They managed, however, to return to these shores having won 15 of their 16 provincial matches and could, with a little luck, have done better in the Tests.

Off the pitch, these tourists were the happiest bunch one could have met, even though some of their high-spirited moments prompted criticism in South African newspapers. There was talk of late night drinking parties and general misbehaviour. Most of the stories were quite untrue and at least appeared to be grossly exaggerated.

In his tour book, On Trek Again, Welsh journalist J. B. G. (Bryn) Thomas categorically denied that they were a "wild bunch".

He accompanied the tour and admitted there were many players who could be described as high- spirited.

But, he stressed, no serious complaints were every made against anyone on the tour and he said most of the sensational stories to emerge were written by pressmen who were not, in fact, travelling with the party and who had got second and third-hand information.

He described the players as "amenable tourists who were never any trouble to anyone off the field".

Kiernan, manager David Brooks and coach Ronnie Dawson appeared to succeed in their aim of quickly blending together players from four different countries and building team sprit. The 1966 tour and its problems were quickly forgotten.

A story told by Irish wing-forward, Mick Doyle, one of eight Irishmen in the party, confirms the determination to achieve that blend: "Syd Millar received a telephone call one night from a former Lions' colleague who had settled in South Africa. He, Tommy Kiernan, Willie John McBride and Ronnie Dawson were invited to his house. Millar refused, saying, 'all of us or nobody'. And they did not go."

It was a pity, then, that with such spirit and determination in the side, they were unable to do better in the series. The third Test proved crucial, for it was here that the Lions could have squared it, and forced the Springboks to wait until the last game for their win.

South Africa won the first match 25-20, when Kiernan kicked five penalties and converted Willie John McBride's try. The second was a draw - 6 points all - but while the Lions went down 6-11 in the third game, they had enough chances to win the game. Instead they lost and the Springboks hammered home their advantage in the last match of the tour by winning handsomely on a 19-6 score line.

It was disheartening certainly, but things may well have taken a turn for the better had not this side been struck with a series of injuries to key players like Barry John, Gerald Davies and Gareth Edwards.

Later on, Ireland's Roger Young was also injured, and that necessitated the call up of Scotland's Gordon Connell who had played just once for his country at that stage. At any rate, their tour average of 15 wins and a draw from 20 games was not disastrous, and was decidedly better than the previous tour to South Africa in 1962.

Kiernan, who did not particularly enjoy himself six years before, emerged as one of the best fullbacks of his time. At times he was criticised at home for rather inconsistent goal kicking, but his ability to score proved a considerable advantage on the hard grounds in South Africa. He was the second highest scorer on the tour, with 84 points, beaten only by England's Bob Hiller who scored 20 more.

The Irishman was a popular choice for the captaincy. Ireland enjoyed an excellent season in the international championship that year and Kiernan was earmarked from the very beginning.

The one threat may have been Welshman John Dawes who, after being dropped by his country, came back to captain the side against Ireland in Lansdowne Road. As it turned out Ireland won and Dawes had to wait until 1971 to become a Lion.

Kiernan regrets that the team were unable to do better, but concedes: "We had a good, but not a great team. South Africa were just too strong for us, although I felt we might have had more success if we had avoided all those injuries."

On tours of this nature, the pressure on players is often overwhelming. A large crowd awaited the arrival of the Lions on 13 May.

Representatives of the press wondered aloud if Kiernan, as captain, had learned some Afrikaans.

"Tell me, Tom", asked one reporter, "do you understand our language?" "Of course I do - provided it's spoken through Irish," was the quick reply. That comment put him at immediate ease with his hosts and set the scene for a fruitful and happy relationship with his players.

Barry Bresnihan of UCD was known throughout the tour as "Doctor", for he was a medical student. A superb tourist, who was well known for his off-the-field renderings of Irish ballads, Bresnihan played in three of the Test matches and in all played 15 times. He also managed to get Mick Doyle drunk for the first time!

95

Kerry-man Doyle, then with Blackrock, was one of the liveliest members of the party, both on and off the pitch. In civvies, he made his presence felt wherever he went and once even introduced himself to a school of performing dolphins in a marine park!

Although a witty character, who likes to look back on the funny side of the tour, Doyle took his rugby very seriously. He had been capped 19 times before embarking on the trip and made a determined bid to secure a test place for himself.

He suffered, however, from a lack of weight and height at the back of a lineout, where he was pitted against much bigger men. He soon made up for these deficiencies and proved himself a most worthy member of the party, playing in eleven matches, including the first Test, when he was vice-captain. He was dropped for the second international, and just as he was clearly challenging again, he sustained an injury struck that put paid to his chances.

Doyle has vivid recollections of the senior member of the playing party, Ballymena's Syd Millar, whom he described as "the old hand - the father figure". Millar, he says, did an immense amount of work to help some of the younger players cope with a tour of such length. "His nick-name was Yogi Bear. He ate honey with his honey, and he came in for a lot of stick because of that. He was one of the fun people, a player's player, who had an enormous influence."

Millar played in nine games and propped in two Tests. That brought his total number of appearances for the Lions to 44 (nine Tests). Having already won 27 caps for Ireland, he went on to play on ten more occasions - only three short of Ray McLoughlin's then Irish record for a prop-forward.

Much was expected of Mike Gibson following his brilliant displays in New Zealand and Australia two years before. Sadly, he failed to "ignite" the Lions as he had done then.

He had his moments, but an injury early on seemed to have blunted much of his enthusiasm and, when he came on as a reserve for the injured Barry John during the first Test, it was clear he was not fully fit.

Later on in the tour, he produced some flashes of magic as only he could do, but as the trip progressed, Gibson's form seemed to regress - not dramatically - but enough to damage the Lions' prospects of tearing South African defences apart. He still made a total of 14 appearances and played in all the Tests.

Roger Young, on his second Lions tour, was chairman of the "scrum-halves union" in South Africa, claiming that he should be the boss because he was older than Welshman Gareth Edwards. The two players became great friends despite the obvious rivalry between them, and so it was a pity to see both eventually injured and out of the running for test places.

It was Edwards who seemed to be winning the duel, getting in for the first two Tests, but then he was stricken with a hamstring injury and Young stepped in for the third. But Young, who had a fine tour, and often took physical punishment without complaint, was denied his second outing against the South Africans as he injured himself a couple of weeks before the final game. Yet he had some considerable success and received acclaim for his performance against Eastern Transvaal, the match that was dubbed "The Battle Of Springs". He scored two tries in nine appearances.

This was Willie John McBride's third Lions tour... and he was not finished yet! McBride made his presence felt in South Africa in a big way and was both feared and respected by the best of the Springboks. The tour was a personal triumph for him, because it was the first one in which he had played in all the Tests. In the latter stages of the trip, McBride was, however, in some trouble, for he tore his leg in the first Test and the wound became poisoned. The injury troubled him subsequently, and to a certain extent hampered him, even though he was still an automatic choice for the Test sides.

Ken Goodall (City of Derry) might well have been an original choice for the tour but he was unavailable because of examinations. However, when Barry John was injured, and it became apparent that he was unlikely to take any further part in the tour, the selectors decided to replace him. The fact that they had only one recognised number eight in the party prompted them, not to look for a back, but for a forward.

His ambition of becoming a Lion realised, Goodall did not last long. During his first game against Eastern Transvaal he broke a bone in his hand, which ruled him out of further activity.

The Irish connection with this tour intensified with the appointment as assistant manager of Ronnie Dawson, who had virtually carte blanche on the coaching side. It was a major breakthrough, for Dawson, captain of the 1959 Lions, was the first man in that position to be given such an opportunity.

1968: SOUTH AFRICA

Played	Won	Drew	Lost	For	Against
20	15	1	4	377	181

Western Transvaal	W	20-12
Western Provinces	W	10-6
South Western District	W	24-6
Eastern Province	W	23-14
Natal	W	17-5
Rhodesia	W	32-6
SOUTH AFRICA	L	20-25
North West Cape	W	25-5
South West Africa	W	23-0
Transvaal	L	6-14
SOUTH AFRICA	D	6-6
Eastern Transvaal	W	37-9
Northern Transvaal	W	22-19
Griqualand West	W	11-3
Boland	W	14-0
SOUTH AFRICA	L	6-11
Border	W	26-6
Orange Free State	W	9-3
North East Cape	W	40-12
SOUTH AFRICA	L	6-19

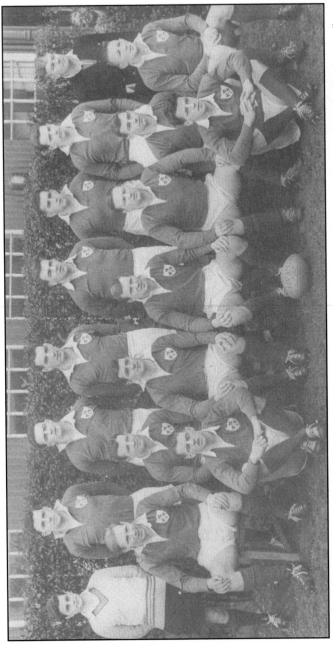

The Irish team which met Scotland in 1960. Ten of the players were Lions at one time or another. Back row (L to r.): Noel Murphy, Bill Mulcahy, Gerry Culliton, Syd Millar, Gordon Wood, Cecil Pedlow. Front row (l. to r.): Tim McGrath, Dave Hewitt, Mick English, Andy Mulligan, Bert McCallan, Wally Bowman, Wally Bowman, Ronnie Kavanagh, On ground: Tom Kiernan and Jerry Walsh.

Ray Hennessey leads out a Presentation Brothers College side for a Munster Schools Cup Final with Rockwell in 1955. Second on the pitch is Irish International and Lion, a very youthful looking Jerry Walsh.

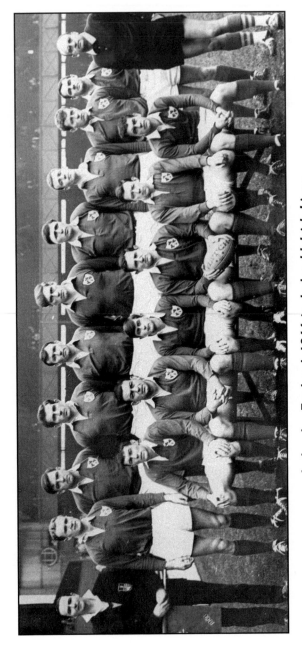

Ireland v. England, 1966 includes 11 Irish Lions.

Mike Gibbon crashes over for a try during the 1966 tour to New Zealand.

Noel Murphy getting the ball away, with Irish players Willie John McBride,
Ronnie Lamount and Ray McLoughlin in the background.

Mick Doyle and Jeff Young escort the injured Roger Young off the field during a 1968 South African encounter.

Willie John McBride in action against Natal in 1968.

CHAPTER 7

THE LIONS ROAR

Carwyn James, who was said to have been symbolic of the swing toward coaching in Britain and Ireland in the late 1960's, proved himself a coach of rare perception, wit and intelligence. John Dawes, surely one of the shrewdest midfield distributors the game has known, kept a firm grip on the exacting job of tour captain. With firmness from management and captain, the team found the depths of character exceeding those of most touring sides. Nor should Ray McLoughlin's technical advice on forward methods early in the tour be forgotten.

Thus the 1971 tour of New Zealand was summed up by a former colleague, David Frost of The Guardian, after the Lions had returned home in triumph, having inflicted upon the All Blacks their first defeat by a touring side since 1937, and having taken the laurels for the first time in that particular part of the Southern Hemisphere.

1971 NEW ZEALAND

McLoughlin, arguably one of the most perceptive front-row forwards of all time, was, however, lost to the tour after a vicious bruising battle against Canterbury, a game that the Lions won 14-

3. In terms of the loss of playing personnel, the win proved very costly. McLoughlin's departure, a short time after the first Test, was described at the time as one of the tragedies of the tour. It was pinpointed very early on that his influence on the forwards, not just as a player, but also as an unofficial coach, had been phenomenal.

The Lions won the series with two victories, a draw and a loss, but there was a general feeling that with McLoughlin present, they would have done even better. Indeed, a suggestion was put forward to allow him to stay on as forward coach, but this did not materialise.

That particular game was one the Lions wanted to forget rather quickly, but how could they? For not only did it spell the end for the classy McLoughlin but it also denied them the services of the established Scottish prop Sandy Carmichael, with Gareth Edwards and then two more Irishmen, Mick Hipwell and Fergus Slattery also having to face treatment for injuries afterwards.

Terenure man Hipwell had a chequered career for Ireland, being first capped in 1962, and then, when it looked as if his international tally would rest at two caps, he was recalled in 1968 when he won two more caps. He got three more in 1969 (twice as a reserve) and was an ever-present in 1971 - perfect timing to help him win a place with the Lions party. In the early part of the tour, Hipwell had been playing so well that he was tipped to get into the Test side but the tragic injury sustained in the Canterbury game was to deny him that honour. He was, along with John Taylor of Wales, selected for the team to meet New Zealand in the first Test, but unfortunately the knee injury kept him out. He remained on with the party in the hope that the injury would heal, but in the week preceding the second Test, he finally had to admit defeat. His injury, diagnosed by three specialists as a torn cartilage in his left knee, ruled him out entirely and so his early potential was not realised. Scotland's loose forward, Roger Arneil, came in as replacement.

Slattery had teeth blown out in that explosive game with Canterbury, but the injury did not stop him from becoming one of the most impressive Lions on the tour. His international career had only begun the season before but by then it was clear that he would be on the scene for a long time. At 21 years of age he made his name quickly in New Zealand, scampering around in the open, bustling his opponents into error and deservedly winning his place for third Test. Like Hipwell, however, there was a sad twist of fate, for he fell ill with a throat infection and had to withdraw from the team. He was forced to wait three years until the triumphant Lions tour to South Africa to win international honours with the Lions.

Sean Lynch, the St Mary's prop forward who went to New Zealand with little hope of making the test team, was thrust into the role of number one because of the injuries sustained by McLoughlin and Carmichael. Lynch was described as "a robust soul" who learned a lot of life running a Dublin pub. Like Carmichael and McLoughlin, Lynch had earlier been involved in incidents. Rather imprudently he held a jersey in a Maori match and the result was a punch in the mouth and 14 stitches. Lynch was an unyielding scrummager but because of a perceived lack of ability at the lineout there was talk of him being replaced by Mike Roberts for the tests.

That did not happen and Lynch made a successful transition from "dirt trekker to Test player virtually overnight. While the other prop forward replacement, Ian McLauchlan, was making a name for himself by scoring a try in the first Test and impressing in the loose, Lynch was getting down to the basic important work of a man in his position - out scrummaging the opposition - and he did so with devastating effect. That was just the start of Lynch's international career that, in addition to the four Lions Tests, was to yield him 17 caps, the last in 1974 against New Zealand.

The now legendary Mike Gibson, who went on the tour as an out-half, settled into the Test side in a different position, such was the form of Barry John, a player more restricted in his ability to change positions.

Gibson was, of course, an automatic choice in the back line, and if the New Zealand fans constantly sang the praises of John more, the general consensus was that Gibson was the man of the tour.

"The Complete Footballer", ran a headline in a newspaper, above an article expounding the virtues of Gibson following the 47-9 thrashing of Wellington. "Gibson's acceleration and deadly chops of direction were one of the main reasons why Wellington was so devastated," said the reporter.

Gibson was sought after by the fans everywhere he went. On the pitch he more often than not got away from his pursuers; off it, he won himself some admiration for the way in which he coped with the adulation. Willie John McBride comments: "I believe thoroughly in the team game. I don't know whether players should be singled out. What I would say is that the 1971 team had a lot of magnificent backs and Mike, in the middle of that, played class rugby." And needless to mention, Gibson was selected for all four Tests and partnered John Dawes in the centre.

Willie John McBride was given the task of leading the pack when Ray McLoughlin was forced out of the tour and it was a challenge to which he responded excellently.

He had his difficulties and conceded then, and many years later, that the series win was in some ways a lucky one. If, three years later, the pack that he led as captain in South Africa were to totally dominate their opponents, the same was not true in New Zealand.

McBride says: "We never dominated them. We stole the first Test when we got a lucky try and kicked two penalties but spent 75 minutes of the game tackling. They thrashed us in the second game. We played well for 20 minutes of the third match, scored 13 points and held on while the fourth game was, as the score line suggests, a very even contest.

But if Mc Bride felt the Lions had their share of luck, he had little or no sympathy for the All Blacks. As he led the team in a victory song, "We Shall Overcome", at the post-match celebrations fol-

108

lowing the 9-3 first Test victory, McBride was probably the most thrilled player of them all. It was McBride's 10th test for the Lions since his debut on the South African tour in 1962 and it was the first time he had been on a winning side. "I have waited so long, too long for this", he announced. A great player, who had given such dedicated service to his country and to the Lions, McBride found a moment of joy in a Test win that set the tourists on the road to that series victory and lifted them out of a wilderness against the All Blacks. The mighty finally got a dose of their own-medicine.

1971: NEW ZEALAND

Played	Won	Drew	Lost	For	Against
26	23	1	2	580	231

Queensland	L	11-15
New South Wales	W	14-12
Counties/Thames Valley	W	25-3
King Country/Wanganui	W	22-9
Waikato	W	35-14
New Zealand Maoris	W	23-12
Wellington	W	47-9
South/Mid~anterbury/North Otago	W	25-6
West Coast/Buller	W	39-6
Canterbury	W	14-3
Marlborough/Nelson Bays	W	31-12
NEW ZEALAND	W	9-3
Southland	W	25-3
Taranaki	W	14-9
New Zealand Universities	W	27-6
NEW ZEALAND	L	12-22
Wairarapa-Bush	W	27-6
Hawkes Bay	W	25-6
Poverty Bay/East Coast	W	18-12
Auckland	W	19-12
NEW ZEALAND	W	13-3
Manawatu/Horowhenua	W	39-6
North Auckland	W	11-5
Bay of Plenty	W	20-14
NEW ZEALAND	D	14-14

1974: SOUTH AFRICA

In 1974, McBride was coming to the end of an illustrious playing career. So when he was honoured with the captaincy of the Lions, it delighted him more than anything that went before, even more than the success in New Zealand.

In almost every Lions tour in modern times there has been some sort of controversy – disagreement at any rate - about the choice of captain. The background to McBride's selection was no different, for there were those who said he was too old at 33 years of age.

He was due to celebrate another birthday in South Africa but he proved that age was no barrier and, based on his performances, there were no signs of mental or physical decay.

Quite simply, McBride was not alone a superb leader, but a magnificent player. By the end of this spectacularly successful tour, he totally confounded his few remaining critics.

The Ballymena hero recalls: "I was well aware of what people were saying, but I'm a queer sort of animal and the bigger the challenge the better I like it."

But he conceded that the success of the tour, during which his team's only blemish was a draw in the final Test (and McBride insists they won that too) was not due to himself:

"The key to that great tour was that each and every player in the party was prepared to die for one another and I personally received absolute loyalty. That to me was tremendous because the party was not a young one. Many of the players were long established internationals, players at the peak of their careers. It gave me great satisfaction that, knowing I was under pressure, they gave everything to ensure that the critics received their answer."

If McBride and coach Millar helped plot the downfall of the South Africans for the first time this century, there were many more who contributed. One of the foremost of these, Fergus

Slattery, probably played better than at any time in his international career, which had begun in 1970.

Slattery, a roving, open-side flanker, with a particular ability to force the opposition into errors - a pressure player - reached, according to McBride, "the peak of the mountain."

McBride continues: "I dislike singling out any player in particular, simply because everyone was good, but Slattery contributed more to the winning of the bigger provincial and Test games than any other player. He was everywhere, was so quick off the mark and he forced more errors amongst South African teams than anyone else."

Slattery played in all four Tests and scored six tries in a total of 12 appearances. That would have amounted to seven, had referee Max Baise awarded him what seemed a perfectly legitimate try in the last minute of the fourth test. The decision cost the Lions a 4-0 series win.

While McBride and Slattery were the only two Irish forwards to partipate in the Test series, the Bangor centre, Dick Milliken, who had been capped 10 times for Ireland up to that time, carved out quite a niche for himself in the centre of the field for the Lions. Milliken, quiet, but yet very determined, struck up an ideal partnership with Ian McGeechan, the Scotsman who later coached the Lions on three overseas tours.

The Ulster player had been living in the shadow of Mike Gibson for his own country, but with Gibson destined not to join the tour until well after it began, Milliken seized his opportunity superbly. Defensively he was most reliable and he proved he could score tries also, running in for five. He made a total of 13 appearances and alongside McGeechan provided huge problems for the South Africans.

A tribute is that even when Gibson arrived in the tour as a replacement for Alan Old and played well, he could not displace his Irish colleague.

Milliken won four more caps for Ireland before a broken leg disrupted his international career.

The non-test Irishmen with the party were Tom Grace and Johnny Moloney, both of St Mary's, Stewart McKinney (Dungannon), Gibson and Ken Kennedy; but the fact that they did not participate in the Test series does not mean they had no role to play. For a start, a decade ago there was no such thing as a medical officer, but Kennedy, being a doctor, was called upon many times during the day and night to administer to the injured. On the field Kennedy distinguished himself, but not enough in 10 appearances to dislodge Bobby Windsor from the hooking spot. Kennedy, like most of the Irish before and after him, was a popular tourist, although some of the referees and linesmen with whom he liked holding conversations might not always have agreed with that!

McKinney's tour appearances were confined to eight, mainly because of injuries, but his penalty goal against Free State, during a game that the Lions won 11-9, proved of vital importance in helping the Lions maintain their unbeaten record. McKinney was reputed to be one of the nicest players in the party and McBride endorses this: "The simplest things in life are probably the most important and are the most noticed at times. I can always remember as captain, the reaction of players when we visited certain places and the one thing you could say about Stewart McKinney was that when leaving, he would be the first person to say thanks to his hosts."

McKinney already had ten caps for Ireland before his tour to South Africa, and he went on to win a further 14 before finally playing his last game in 1978 against England.

Mike Gibson was unavailable for the tour at the outset, but he had intimated to the selectors that he would be willing to replace any injured player towards the end of June if the need arose. And so when Alan Old was the victim of a late tackle in a match against Proteas, he was called for. At 31 years of age, he had already been on three Lions tours, but this time there was no displacing Milliken or McGeechan in the centre. He was confined, therefore, to seven

113

provincial matches, but he played very well in these and scored two tries as well as kicking a conversion.

His Lions appearances were not over, for he also travelled with the party to New Zealand three years later and in fact did not retire from international rugby until 1979.

Johnny Moloney, one of two St Mary's men in the side, had a disastrous start to the tour, dislocating his shoulder in the first match against Western Transvaal. That was the initial problem. The second was Gareth Edwards and even a fit Moloney would have conceded that his chances of gaining a Test place would have been remote anyway. That injury and hamstring trouble towards the end of the tour confined him to eight outings, yet, in the matches he played, he did well. He scored three fine tries and displayed his qualities as a fast breaking half, an aspect of his play that severely troubled the opposition.

Grace took some time to impact on the tour. He failed to make the Test team, yet he struck form to become a prolific try scorer. When the tour ended he had scored 13 times in 11 appearances, one more than his archrival but friend, J. J. Williams, who commanded a Test position right through the series. That was some compensation at least for failing to win a place in the international games.

The 1974 tour was yet another example of the Irish contribution to Lions rugby over the years. McBride and coach Syd Millar, both of whom had worked in close co-operation with each other for some time before on the home scene, moulded together an all-conquering side that McBride later described as something akin to a machine.

"It was like something you turned on and off. You switched it on the morning of a game and off afterwards, so that the players not alone won their matches but also thoroughly enjoyed their visit to South Africa. The players were just not going to be beaten and Syd, I believe, had a great deal to do with that.

"We had both been to South Africa before and knew something about the strength of the game there. That was a bonus. Syd and I both believe that rugby is about doing the simple things well. If one succeeds in doing that at this level, all the other natural skills and abilities fall into place, and he had the knack of encouraging players to allow those skills come to the surface.

"But while we worked well as a team, it must also be said that 1974 was a good time in the four countries as far as rugby playing strength was concerned. Looking at the team before we left, it seemed very promising and in hindsight we did not have injury problems.

"We played four tests with just 17 players so there were some things which ran well for us. We had a fine pack, which was able to dominate the Springboks and the backs; all of them with inherent skills took it from there.

I believe another thing that helped us in South Africa was the fact we were very much on our own. I was under a certain amount of pressure, but so was the rest of the party because of the political situation. Nobody at home really wanted us to be there and so we knew if we wanted to survive it had to be through our own efforts. Syd did more than anyone to instil that determination in the players."

From the very first games, these Lions made an impact with a succession of impressive victories in the build up to the first Test. Those wins included a 97-0 drubbing of South West Districts.

After they won the first and second Tests, they continued to go on scoring sprees throughout the countryside. Only Orange Free State (11-9) and Northern Transvaal (16-12) ever came too close to this team for comfort.

While politicians of the day might not have been happy to see the tour go ahead, there appeared to be no complaints afterwards!

1974: SOUTH AFRICA

Played	Won	Drew	Lost	For	Against
22	21	1	0	729	207

Western Transvaal	W	59-13
South West Africa	W	23-16
Boland	W	33-6
Eastern Province	W	28-14
South-West Districts	W	97-0
Western Province	W	17-8
Proteas	W	37-6
SOUTH AFRICA	W	12-3
Southern Universities	W	26-4
Transvaal	W	23-15
Rhodesia	W	42-6
SOUTH AFRICA	W	28-9
Quaggas	W	20-16
Orange Free State	W	11-9
Griqualand West	W	69-16
Northern Transvaal	W	16-12
African Leopards	W	56-10
SOUTH AFRICA	W	26-9
Border	W	26-6
Natal	W	34-6
Eastern Transvaal	W	33-10
SOUTH AFRICA	D	13-13

Captain Fantastic Willie John McBride in his leadership role in 1974 and in action for the Lions

Mike Gibson, five times a Lions tourist, foiled as he tries to blast through another defence

CHAPTER 8

DEFEAT -AGAIN

The strains of touring were bound to take their toll. The Lions, having gained series wins in New Zealand and South Africa in 1971 and 1974, travelled once again to meet the All Blacks in 1977, but they had to do so without a few Players who might well have made a difference.

Welshman Graham Price was making his Lions debut on that tour and in 1983, while making his third trip with the Lions, he made some pertinent remarks about the sacrifices which players had to make in order to tour. Price was critical of the Home Rugby Unions for the way in which members of a Lions tour group were treated at that time.

He referred to the weekly wage allowance that the players received and, while agreeing that the nominal sum was "fair enough because the players were getting paid by their employers anyway", suggested that the Unions should relieve the various companies of the burden they had to endure.

It would be much easier, Price said, for players of the this calibre to go on Lions tours if they could approach employers and ask for unpaid leave, with the Rugby Unions left to foot the subsequent bill.

It was because of their reluctance to do so that players such as Gareth Edwards, J. P R. Williams, Mervyn Davies and Fergus Slattery were unable to travel, claimed Price.

1977: NEW ZEALAND AND FIJI

The 1977 tour was not the happiest in some respects apart from results.

The Lions lost the test series 1-3; the management team of Scotsman George Burrell and John Dawes of Wales became lonely figures by the end of the trip; and dreadful weather contributed to the misery of the tour.

English hooker Peter Wheeler managed to keep his sanity, however, and in a letter home a few weeks before the conclusion of the tour, wittily wrote: "Good news, it has only rained twice this week, once for three days, once for four days." That comment just about summed up the general feeling about the meteorological situation.

Although the tour was dogged by bad weather, the Lions came close to winning the Test series or at least drawing it. They lost the first test 12-16 after All Black winger Grant Batty got an oppor-tunist try. They won the second game, but lost the next two, the last by just one point. The 1977 Lions played 26 games, scored 607 points and conceded 320.

Yet, despite all the problems, there were lively moments and many of them concerned the Irishmen in the side. The original selection included just three from Ireland - Phil Orr, Willie Duggan and Mike Gibson - but Moss Keane, or "Rent-a-Storm" as he became known on the trip, joined the party prior to their departure, when he replaced the injured Geoff Wheel.

As always, Keane, the great contributor, both on and off the pitch, made his presence felt early on. To other nationalities, Moss may be difficult to understand. Manager Burrell was one of them and there are reports of hilarious conversations between the two men.

In one, frustration finally got the better of the Irishman and he turned to Burrell saying: "George, for God's sake, am I talking too fast, or are you listening too slow?"

Moss was a bit of a hell raiser, but in a good--humoured sort of way. He has never done any real harm apart from perhaps ripping a few shirts. He had a burning desire to see buttons popping!

Speaking of burning, no hotels were set on fire or anything during the 1977 tour, but the Fire Brigade were alerted on several occasions. Moss felt they should be out there doing something and so he and others conveniently arranged for them to be given a bit of overtime. Invariably, however, when they got to the destination of the fire, it had been a false alarm. The Kerry man won himself such a reputation for this type of prank that when a "Court" session - a regular occurrence on tours of this nature - was arranged, Moss was appointed judge, but instead of being garbed in a cloak, his colleagues presented him with a fireman's hat!

Graham Price recalls Keane's hatred of flying: "I shared a flight with him in 1977 from Palmerston North to Blenheim and Moss was terrified. He sat there with his left hand gripped to the seat in front of him as we made our way down the runway, and then I saw something, which I have never seen before, or since. He picked this bottle of whiskey out of his bag with one hand, opened it with one hand and drank from it. All the time his other hand was clutched to the seat."

There was, and is, a more serious side to Moss Keane, and although he failed to hold his Test place in New Zealand, having played alongside Allan Martin in the first, he still had a fairly successful tour. While only playing five times in nine weeks after that opening Test, Keane maintained his sense of purpose, and, of course, his humour.

From the playing point of view, Willie Duggan was the most successful of the Irish, winning a place at number eight in all four Tests, and if he neglected to take a scoring chance in the last minute

121

of the fourth Test, which would probably have won the match, his all-round performances on the tour cannot be faulted. He was one of the outstanding forwards of the side and was respected by opponents and admired by his own players.

Duggan's determination was always evident and he was able to soak up punishment without complaining. Graham Price recalls his playing against the New Zealand Maoris. "He was the only number eight in a position to play, even though he should have been rested, having received punishment in a previous match. His back was virtually raw and to protect himself he was almost encased in padding. He was like a man with a parachute on his back going onto the pitch. Yet he never made it through the game. Some guy discovered that he had no padding on his face and hit him!"

Duggan was not short on wit either. Like Keane, he did not particularly relish the thought of training. The team's hotel in Christchurch had an elevator that regularly broke down. As the team awaited a bus to take them training one morning, Duggan and a few others were missing. trapped in the lift. Somebody managed to prise open the door on another level wide enough to speak to them and he shouted: "It will be OK in a few minutes lads, we're getting somebody to fix the lift".

Back came a prompt reply from Duggan: "We're not going anywhere. Just send us down some beer and sandwiches!"

Mike Gibson was, at 34 years of age, the oldest playing member of the party. The magical genius that he produced for Ireland, and for previous Lions teams, were missing on this occasion, however, although he occasionally played inspired rugby. He was out of form in the early stages, but just when it looked as though he was improving, he suffered a hamstring injury. These two factors contrived to keep him out of the Test sides, but he can still boast that he was the only player in the party not to have been on a losing side. In all, he played 11 games.

Some of the press party on the 1977 tour were of the opinion that Phil Orr, the long-serving Irish loose head prop, was treated shabbily.

Orr played in the first Test that the Lions were unlucky to lose, and he was said to have had a fine game. Yet he lost his place to Fran Cotton and only played in four more games out of 16. His scrummaging was controlled and in the loose he had a fine tour. If he had been allowed more matches, he might well have re--established himself as the loose head. Instead, he was destined to sit on the bench no less than 11 times after that opening Test.

1977 : NEW ZEALAND AND FIJI

Played	Won	Drew	Lost	For	Against
26	21	0	5	607	320

Wairarapa Bush		W	41-13
Hawkes Bay		W	13-11
Poverty Bay/East Coast		W	25-6
Taranaki		W	21-13
King Country/Wanganui		W	60-9
Manawatu/Horowhenui		W	18-12
Otago		W	12-7
Southland		W	20-12
New Zealand Universities		L	9-21
NEW ZEALAND		L	12-16
South Canterbury/Mid Canterbury			
North Otago		W	45-6
Canterbury		W	14-13
West Coast/Buller		W	45-0
Wellington		W	13-6
Marlborough/Nelson Bay		W	40-23
NEW ZEALAND		W	13-9
New Zealand Maoris		W	22-19
Waikato		W	18-13
New Zealand Juniors		W	19-9
Auckland		W	34-15
NEW ZEALAND		L	7-19
Counties/Thames Valley		W	35-10
North Auckland		W	18-7
Bay of Plenty		W	23-15
NEW ZEALAND		L	9-10
Fiji		L	21-25

1980: SOUTH AFRICA

The 1980 tour to South Africa will go down in history as the most injury-ridden tour of all time. If the Lions thought they had problems with the rain of New Zealand in 1977, it was nothing to the difficulties encountered on the hard pitches of South Africa when, after the tour began, eight replacement or additional players had to be called for.

The Lions battle plan was disrupted time and time again as the spate of injuries began and continued. It was at times like Emergency Ward Ten. Welshmen Elgin Rees (an eve of tour replacement for Andy Irvine), Gareth Williams and Ian Stephens, Englishmen Paul Dodge and Steve Smith, Irish players Tony Ward, John Robbie and Phil Orr, plus Irvine himself, were all called for at various stages of the tour.

Five Irish players were originally selected: Rodney O'Donnell (St Mary's), Ollie Campbell (Old Belvedere), Colin Patterson (Instonians), John O'Driscoll (London Irish) and Colm Tucker (Shannon); but before the end of the tour the selection jumped to eight with the arrival of Ward, Robbie and Orr. In addition, they were managed by an Irishman - Syd Millar - and coached by an Irishman - Noel Murphy - both former Lions themselves.

Despite all the trials of the 1980 Lions, it is generally acknowledged that theirs was a more successful tour than that of 1977, even if they lost the Test series by the same margin.

Millar initially turned down the opportunity to take the job as manager but then changed his mind.

A veteran of tours to South Africa, one with Ireland in 1961, two with the Lions in 1962 and 1968 as a player, one as coach with the all-conquering 1974 Lions side and another as coach to a Rest of the World party to celebrate the opening of the new Loftus Versfeld stadium in Pretoria, Millar was just about the most experienced man around for the job.

Management brings with it a certain amount of responsibility that, if not tackled properly, can provide touring sides with major problems.

But the players thought very highly of Millar, a straight talker who did not pull any punches.

Graham Price says of him: "If he had something to say to a player, he just came straight out and said it. It might not have been always complimentary, but that type of approach is fair enough. Players sometimes need to be protected and Millar was great at ensuring we had our privacy when we needed it. Apart from that, he was a good manager."

Millar and Murphy played 17 times for the Lions between them, a total equal to that of Willie John McBride's record. To some, the Millar-Murphy combination may have been strange, given the fact that Millar is a North of Ireland Protestant and Murphy a Catholic from the South. Some jokes were made of the fact that the squad was announced on 17 March and the last Test was played on 12 July.

Of course, their union was not strange at all, because in Ireland there are few problematic barriers in rugby circles. Protestants and Catholics, North and South, have all been playing rugby under the one banner for over 100 years and it is unlikely that this will ever change.

Murphy is a tee-totaller, but has been known to act "drunk" in a party mood. In the 1980 tour he was just as much involved in players' activities as he was in management's. According to Price, "he was just one of us". But while Murphy's drinks were non-alcoholic, it is a fact that once on tour he did get tipsy. While celebrating a victory one evening, Murphy was indulging in his favourite minerals. He was completely unaware that his drinks were being laced with vodka in increasing amounts as the night went on. The following morning he complained of a severe headache, but to this day he insists that the alleged mischief could not have happened. The players insist that it did.

The biggest surprise choice for the tour was surely Colm Tucker, the big Shannon flanker, who had played just twice for Ireland, once as a reserve. But Tucker established himself long before the end of the tour and played a dynamic role in the last two Tests, helping the Lions to a victory in the fourth. This was the first and only time that South Africa lost a final Test game to the Lions.

The Lions lacked a flying wing-forward on that tour and Tucker seemed to be the only one to help them out, even though he was forced to play a role he may not have been suited to. In the circumstances he did tremendously well and was one of the big successes of the tour.

Maurice Colclough, the big English second row, spent a lot of time in the company of John O'Driscoll on the tour, but very rarely met his "friend". O'Driscoll is the quiet man of rugby, friendly and serious. But there is a fun side to him and that is why Colclough referred to him as "O'Driscoll and friend" – the friend being a different side of his personality.

In South Africa, O'Driscoll was regarded as one of the most consistent members of the party, being rewarded with a place in each of the four Tests and scoring a try in two of them - the only one to do so.

The tour was to end in tragedy for impish Irish scrum- half Colin Patterson who, after the injury to Welshman Terry Holmes, established himself as number one.

In any event, Patterson received some rave reviews for his performances and he played in three tests, before he received a catastrophic knee injury in the last game prior to the final Test. Patterson, the smallest and lightest player, was forced to give up his job as a solicitor to make the tour.

His employers complained so much when he toured Australia the previous year that he decided there was no point in asking for leave for 10 weeks. It was to prove costly in more ways than one, for the injury, which was said at the time to be the most serious ever of that type, left his international career in ruins.

Ollie Campbell had his share of injury problems too and was ruled out of eight of the first nine matches because of hamstring trouble. But the golden touch was still there when he did play, and he scored in all but one of his appearances, the exception being in the second Test when he came on as a replacement for Gareth Davies. Campbell was, predictably, the tour's top scorer with 60 points, and that was achieved despite the fact that he had been injured for so long.

A great admirer of Campbell's on that tour was Clive Woodward, who accredited Campbell with some of his own scoring success. Woodward finished second to Campbell with a total of 53 points that included five conversions and eight penalties. The English-man said at the time: "Campbell taught me that successful goal kicking was all about getting the run-up correct."

Reserve John Robbie was unique in that he was the only player to line out in a Test who did not play on a losing side. He appeared on seven occasions and had an exceptionally good test. He scored seven points, which he achieved through a try and a drop goal in the second last game of the tour, against Griqualand West.

Phil Orr had a quiet tour and while he played five games, he appeared only in one Saturday match. Although Tony Ward was dropped to the mid-week side and only got five games, he still won a Test place for the opening match and went into history by scoring a record 18 points in the first test.

The Irish, it has been said, time and time again, are colourful tourists, but in 1980, Rodney O'Donnell must surely have beaten the lot of them. O'Donnell was notoriously superstitious. He was a talking point before the group ever left London and was constantly the butt of pranks by his fellow players. On the rugby pitch, O'Donnell would always take care to step over, rather than on, straight lines, and if the opposition scored a penalty or a goal of another nature, he would always throw the ball back over the crossbar.

Off the pitch, if he trod on a line, he would re-trace his steps. Getting into bed turned out to be a rare ritual: all wall hangings had to be perfectly straight and the bed covers folded back. Then he would charge onto the bed, taking care not to touch the bed covers, and hitting the bottom sheet first. He always refused to take a room where the numbers added up to 13 and was horrified on Friday 13 June when his colleagues decided to play a joke on him.

When he left his room, they plastered the number 13 all over the door and they chalked straight lines all over the floor of the corridor. To make his exit impossible, they replaced the various numbers on the lift with the number 13. O'Donnell immediately retreated back to his room and told them they would have to carry him out.

That, in the end, is what happened!

O'Donnell won a place in the team for the first Test, and although dropped for the second, was still in contention for a place.

However, an injury received against the Junior Springboks in the 12th match of the tour put paid to his aspirations. While tackling one of the opposition, he damaged his neck, and the injury was so serious that it forced him to retire early from the game.

1980 SOUTH AFRICA

Played	Won	Drew	Lost	For	Against
18	15	0	3	401	244

Eastern Province	W	28-16
South Africa Rugby Association Invitation team	W	28-6
Natal	W	21-15
South African Invitation XV	W	22-19
Orange Free State	W	21-17
SARF Invitation XV	W	15-6
SOUTH AFRICA	L	22-26
South Africa Country XV	W	27-7
Transvaal	W	32-12
Eastern Transvaal	W	21-15
SOUTH AFRICA	L	19-26
Junior Springboks	W	17-6
Northern Transvaal	W	16-9
SOUTH AFRICA	L	10-12
South African Barbarians	W	25-14
Western Province	W	37-6
Griqualand West	W	23-19
SOUTH AFRICA	W	17-13

112

Irish No. 8 Willie Duggan looks for support during the Lions' match against Auckland in 1977.d

Moss Keane in action against England. He was on 1977 Tour.

English prop forward Gary Pearce under attack as Ciaran Fitzgerlad and Willie Duggan prepare for the execution. And more help is on its way! All three Irishmen were Lions.

132

Tony Ward, 1980 Lion, in action for Munster against the All Blacks in Limerick in 1978; His inch perfect kick led to a Munster try which spurred them on to a famous 12-0 victory.

Noel Murphy, John O'Driscoll and Phill Orr relax on the 1980 tour to South Africia.

The Munster Team that beat Australia in 1981 included Five Lions - Gerry McLoughlin, Donal Lenihan, Colm Tucker, Michael Kiernan and Tony Ward.

CHAPTER 9

BULLETS AND FLAK JACKETS

THE early 1980's could be described as a golden era for Irish rugby, ranking alongside the closing years of the 19th century and the latter stages of the 1940's as well.

The forwards in the teams of 1982 and 1983 were affectionately known as "Dad's Army", based on their age profile. All of them, apart from Donal Lenihan, were close to or past the 30 mark. The backs were younger, but while some of them lacked experience they were all highly motivated players.

For the first time in years, the Irish selectors found a top quality blend of experience and class and they marched to glory by winning the Triple Crown for the first time since 1949.

The history of Irish rugby is littered with examples of one-off victories and decent one-off seasons.

Those who hoped Ireland would be well represented on the Lions tour to New Zealand in 1983 wondered whether the progress could be sustained into the 1982/1983 season.

In recent years and particularly in 2001, the Five or Six Nations Championship has not been the only yardstick that Lions selectors judge candidates. In the professional era, players are watched over and over again in various domestic competitions

136

and, of course, in the Heineken European Cup. The Championship is very important but not everything.

In 1983, those who performed usually won a bigger representation than those who didn't.

Ireland, under captain Ciaran Fitzgerald, set out in pursuit of further achievement by winning the opening games of the championship against Scotland and France. Talk of a Grand Slam was in the air when they travelled to Cardiff only for the Irish to come unstuck.

Having done so much for personal and collective glory up to then, it all came down to the last game against England at Lansdowne Road.

The players were surely thinking ahead to Auckland and it was an especially important game for Fitzgerald. He and English hooker Peter Wheeler were battling for the captaincy.

The view was that if Wheeler won, Fitzgerald wouldn't even make the trip. If Fitzgerald won, Wheeler certainly would.

As events transpired, Ireland stormed to a 25-10 victory that day. They ripped the English rearguard to shreds and set the scene for a hugely interesting Lions selection meeting just two days later on Monday, March 21.

Ireland's win over England helped them to a share of the championship and swung the balance of power Fitzgerald's way. Wheeler even lost out on selection and the second hooker named in the party was Colin Deans.

The squad was pretty evenly balanced in terms of nationality with eight Irish, eight Welsh, eight Scots and six English amongst the 30 players selected.

Fitzgerald was named alongside Hugo MacNeill, Trevor Ringland, Michael Kiernan, David Irwin, Ollie Campbell, Donal Lenihan and John O'Driscoll.

It could have been more. Phil Orr, Fergus Slattery and Willie Duggan would all have been live candidates but had made themselves unavailable due to work commitments.

As it transpired, Lenihan never made it at the start. He failed a medical examination because of a minor condition but was eventually called out on tour as a replacement. The arrival of Gerry McLoughlin as a further replacement pushed the Irish representation up to nine before the end of the tour.

The captaincy, due to feelings within small but influential sections of the English media, was a major talking point and a controversial issue from the start right through to the finish of this 1983 tour.

The knives were drawn from as early as the second game against Auckland when an injury time drop goal by the then teenage Grant Fox gave the home side a 13-12 win.

The criticism peaked from the first Test onwards; a match, which the Lions were desperately unlucky to lose 16-12, and Fitzgerald appeared to be constantly in the firing line.

Those were the days, of course, of the longer tour and it embraced four Tests over a period of six weeks. It's a long time to have to reflect when things are not going your way.

At one stage, having endured a printed battering, Army Officer Fitzgerald rang his brother in Ireland and asked him to send out an Army flak jacket. Over the telephone he explained: "The one I have with me is riddled with bullets!"

Quite how Fitzgerald had to shoulder the blame for the 4-0 series loss was beyond the comprehension of a lot of more fair-minded people, broadsheet journalists from both Britain and New Zealand in particular.

Many knowledgeable rugby personalities spoke, for instance about some deficiencies amongst the line out jumpers. Maurice Colclough started the tour in recovery from a serious knee injury and never played at his best. Welshman Bob Norster had a back strain that ruled him out of the last two Tests. Steve Boyle (England) simply wasn't up to it and Steve Bainbridge found the going tough when thrown in at the deep end.

By the time Lenihan was called out, it was too late to challenge for a place.

Daily Telegraph journalist John Mason described the situation like this: "I cannot subscribe to the well publicised theory that the bulk of the problems can be laid at the ever open door of Ciaran Fitzgerald. Under persistent provocation, he maintained a dignified calm, although he must have been seething at some of the wounding barbs delivered with all the charity of a posse of piranha fish. Cast the scales from your eyes, this is a game, not an inquisition!"

New Zealand Times journalist Alex Vesey, in his summation of the tour, brought up the subject of Fitzgerald's worth to the side when he suggested it was a traditional type of division on Lions tours.

"I could understand the host nation trying to divide and conquer but it was the English media, who should have been more supportive at the beginning at least, that caused most of the problems.

"The Fitzgerald/Colin Deans debate was a matter of insignificance compared with the lack of planning and the defensiveness with which the Lions approached the two vital Tests, the first and second."

Certainly, the Lions management, Ireland's Willie John McBride, Scotland's Jim Telfer and Fitzgerald (you would wonder whether he had any influence in selecting the team) made a glaring error when naming the team for the first Test.

Michael Kiernan had won widespread praise all over New Zealand for his play in previous games and was looked upon as a major threat. Yet, the outside centre position was filled by inside centre Rob Ackerman of Wales, a fine player but one who lacked Kiernan's pace.

In the circumstances, Ackerman had a fair enough game but lost a golden opportunity to score a try towards the end of the first half by cutting inside with men outside him.

In a Test series, you don't do anything to give the host nation the initiative. The Lions did by excluding Kiernan and they paid the price. From there, it was an uphill and vain struggle.

The first three Tests were good contests and the Lions, had they taken opportunities, could have won two of them, the first and third. The last is best forgotten because, with the series beyond them, they were flattened by a classic All Black performance.

There was some consolation for the Irish at any rate because win, lose or draw, the honour of playing Test rugby for the Lions can never be taken away.

All seven players who started the tour got a crack at it and Lenihan, had he not been rashly despatched home by team doctor Donald McLeod, would surely have got his chance as well.

Fitzgerald and Campbell played in all four, Irwin, Kiernan and MacNeill (one as substitute) in three, O'Driscoll in two and Ringland in one.

Campbell was one of the shining lights of this Lions party and finished as top scorer with 124 points, well ahead of England's Dusty Hare. Included in that total was one of the best tries ever seen in international rugby – against Waikato in he second last match of the tour.

Having deservedly established his place for the first two, MacNeill lost form and his confidence was wrecked when forced to unsuccessfully attempt to kick the Lions to victory against Ranfurly Shield holders Canterbury four days before the third Test. The Lions lost 22-20 and MacNeill, an erstwhile goal-kicker, missed a succession of chances.

Gwyn Evans of Wales took over but MacNeill did come on as substitute in the last game of the tour.

Desperate measures were needed for the third Test and, for the first time, the selection made it look like the Lions wanted to attack.

Irwin lost out to John Rutherford and John O'Driscoll to Jim Calder. Rutherford was a class act but had to sit out the first two games because of Campbell's top form, and he deserved a chance at this level based on his own displays in previous matches.

The selection of Calder was altogether more controversial although one could sense what the selectors were trying to do. The Scotsman was an open side flanker and he was paired with Peter Winterbottom. The hope was that between the two the Lions might win more ball on the deck.

Sadly, the ploy didn't work and that was probably because of the day that was in it. Rain poured down for days before the game in Dunedin and conditions made it impossible to play either controlled or destructive rugby. It was, in fact, a lottery and the All Blacks won it!

The Lions outscored the All Blacks on the try count 2-1 but still came out at the wrong end of a 15-8 score line in this game, a game that became known as the "vest and mittens" international.

The reason for it is the fact that the All Blacks management purchased diving vests and special mittens to keep the players as warm as humanly possible in atrocious wet and freezing conditions. It was a game that in ordinary circumstances should never have been played.

Rutherford made an impact and scored one of the two tries but was subsequently injured and that paved the way for Irwin's return for the fourth Test.

The lack of success with the back row experiment also gave O'Driscoll the chance to claim his place in the side for the last match but it didn't make any difference as New Zealand romped to an easy win.

Kiernan had a fine Test series and was up there with the best of the Lions backs, even as they suffered from a lack of quality possession in the series. Ringland had to be happy with a Test place for the opening match and it was no shame that he gave way to the more experienced English winger John Carleton who scored nine tries, more than anyone else, throughout the tour.

As the Lions trudged home, there were a lot of bitterly disappointed young men. All admitted they were not good enough but most believed they had also under-achieved.

The reasons for the drubbing were far more varied than "problems" with the captain. There was, as already stated, some poor selection, a bit of bad luck at crucial stages of the tour, injury difficulties with key players and the acceptance of an itinerary that even New Zealanders described as crazy.

Still, the Lions of '83 played a lot of good rugby and won many friends for that.

1983 RESULTS

Played	Won	Drew	Lost	For	Against
18	12	0	6	478	276

Wanganui	W	47-15
Auckland	L	12-13
Bay of Plenty	W	34-16
Wellington	W	27-19
Manawatu	W	25-18
Mid Canterbury	W	26-6
NEW ZEALAND	L	12-16
West Coast	W	52-16
Southland	W	41-3
Wairarapa-Bush	W	57-10
NEW ZEALAND	L	0-9
North Auckland	W	21-12
Canterbury	L	20-22
NEW ZEALAND	L	8-15
Hawkes Bay	W	25-19
Counties	W	25-16
Waikato	W	40-13
NEW ZEALAND	L	6-38

143

1986:
INTERNATIONAL BOARD CENTENARY GAME
IN CARDIFF

The Lions had been due to tour South Africa in 1986 but the schedule was broken when the Four Home Unions bowed to public pressure because of apartheid.

That came as a disappointment to the players even though many of them were in full agreement with the decision at the time.

Instead, it was decided to hold a game between the Lions and the Rest of the World in Cardiff as part of the Centenary celebrations of the International Rugby Board. It was the first time the Lions played at home and the players who participated in the game were given full Lions status.

Clive Rowlands was named as manager and Ireland's Mick Doyle, who plotted Ireland's 1985 Triple Crown win, was coach.

There were five Irish players in the team and another on the bench, suggesting that Ireland would have had a significant presence in a 30-man squad had the tour gone ahead.

Trevor Ringland was the only Irish survivor from the Test teams of 1983 but he was joined by Donal Lenihan, who had been so unlucky three years previously. Brendan Mullin won a place in the side alongside Welsh youngster John Devereux, while Des Fitzgerald and Nigel Carr were named in the pack with Lenihan. Michael Kiernan was chosen as one of the six reserves but was not called upon.

It was a closely contested game, but once again the mainly southern hemisphere side, with a little help from three French players, prevailed and won the game 15-7.

British and Irish Lions 7 (J. Beattie try, G. Hastings penalty) Rest of the World 15 (N. Farr-Jones, S. Poidevan try each, M. Lynagh penalty, 2 conversions).

144

Lions: G. Hastings (Scotland), T. Ringland (Ireland), B. Mullin (Ireland), J. Devereux (Wales), R. Underwood (England), J. Rutherford (Scotland), R. Jones (Wales), J. Whitefoot (Wales), C. Deans (Scotland) captain; D. Fitzgerald (Ireland), D. Lenihan (Ireland), W. Dooley (England), J. Jeffrey (Scotland), J. Beattie (Scotland), N. Carr (Ireland). Substitutes. M. Dacey (Wales) for Rutherford, I. Paxton (Scotland) for Dooley. Other substitutes – M. Kiernan (Ireland), R. Hill (England), I. Milne (Scotland), S. Brain (England).

Michael Kiernan in action against Wellington 1983.

Gerry McLoughlin - Replacement Prop in 1983.

Trevor Ringland, the most improved back in 1983, scored many important tries for the Lions.

Ollie Campbell, the Irish goal-kicking maestro - one player who did not fail to live up to his reputation on tour in 1983.

147

The artistry of Ollie Campbell in evidence as he weaves his way past Steve Pokere and Ian Dunn in the first test of the 1983 New Zealand tour in Christchurch, David Irwin and Peter Winterbottom are the other Lions players

Donal Lenihan in flying form at Hawkes Bay.

Crocks' corner! Nigel Melville, Jeff Squire and Ian Stephens pose with Trevor Ringland, Jim Calder, Michael Kiernan, Graham Price and team physiotherapist, Kevin Murphy.

Captain Ciaran Fitzgerald flanked by Graham Price and Ian Stephens

CHAPTER 10

SCARLET HEAVEN

IT was the first time in 90 years for the Lions to exclusively tour Australia. Yes, they did take on the Wallabies on seven occasions over four trips down under in the intervening years but always in tandem with a series against New Zealand as well.

The record was impressive. Having lost the first Test in 1899, the Lions went on to win the series 3-1. Their only other defeat by Australia came in 1930, and over a total of 14 games the Lions emerged victorious in 12.

But in 1989, the order of rugby had begun to change. The drums were beating and native Australians were getting restless. They were tired of being looked upon as the poor relations of southern hemisphere rugby, and were already in the planning stages of launching a serious assault on the Rugby World Cup of 1991.

As it transpired, they were successful in that bid, but they could never have known then that it would have to take a last minute victory over Ireland in a Lansdowne Road quarter-final to spur them on to greatness.

This Lions tour was a real testing ground for the emerging Wallabies and the Lions were struck by the ferocity of their play in the opening Test which the home side so easily won.

In terms of representation, it wasn't a good year for the Irish. Four players made the trip - Paul Dean, Brendan Mullin, Steve Smith and Donal Lenihan - and only one of them played at the highest level.

Paul Dean's tour was over almost before it began. He had been one of Ireland's most consistent performers over the previous few seasons and got into the tour party ahead of England's Rob Andrew.

Dean was picked for the opening game against Western Australia in Perth, a match the Lions won with lots of points to spare, but unfortunately sustained a leg injury that ended his participation in the tour. He stayed with the party until after the third game against Queensland in Brisbane but was then replaced by Andrew who later went on to become one of the stars of the tour.

Mullin was the chosen one for Test status but suffered because of the Lions' inability to win the first of the three big matches.

He partnered Mike Hall of Wales in that first match and in the context of the game did not play badly. Unfortunately, the Lions were battered into submission by an in-form Wallaby pack and the home back division, particularly Nick-Farr Jones and Michael Lynagh hammered home that advantage.

At least, Mullin didn't feel isolated as a result of his exclusion for the remaining Tests. Hall, Craig Chalmers of Scotland, Robert Norster (Wales) and Derek White (Scotland) were also axed.

The changes made had the desired affect as the Lions went on to take the series with back to back victories in Brisbane and Sydney over the following two weekends.

While neither Smith nor Lenihan ever appeared to have a realistic chance of making the side, it is not to say that they didn't make a huge contribution.

In Lenihan's case it was staggering and he received due recognition from all quarters during and after the tour.

The midweek side were affectionately known as Donal's Doughnuts and the Cork man captained them throughout their own personal campaign.

The presence in the party of Paul Ackford and Wade Dooley, two of England's heavyweight second rows, meant that Lenihan was left mostly to team up with Norster, the man he should have partnered in the 1983 Test team in New Zealand.

Welsh winger Ieuan Evans, a man who made a major impact on the 1989 tour when his smash and grab try was crucial as the Lions won the third Test 19-18, believes Lenihan contributed as much as anyone in the Saturday team.

"You cannot over-estimate the value of what that midweek side did on that tour. After the first Test, we were struggling big time and we had to pull ourselves together. Donal's side really dragged us through it.

"After losing that first game in Sydney, we had to go down to Canberra and Donal's lot took on ACT. At half time, they were out cold but came back to win. After that, we gained the motivation and re-discovered the spirit needed to take on Australia."

Another Welshman on that tour was Robert Jones and he concurred with Evans on his views about Lenihan.

"I have never experienced anything like that 1989 tour where everyone worked together. Training sessions were what you might call tasty. There was a real competitive edge to them but once the Test sides were chosen, the guys who lost out went out of their way to congratulate the winners.

"It was only after the second Test that guys could relax a bit and feel they were going to get in for the final one.

"That year, we were away for nine weeks and it was a long haul. When you have a group of players living and eating together for so long, you need people to pull everyone together.

"Donal was one of those people with a special gift for being able to do that. He was funny, enjoyed himself but had only one thing in mind really - and that was to get on with the job of helping the Lions win every match they played. He was strong willed, motivated and hard. His very presence there was enough to make everyone stand up and get on with it.

"Nobody ever got too far out of line because there were people like Finlay Calder and Donal who had been around a long time and were very much part and parcel amongst the senior set up in the squad. Because of that, things never broke up. It always stayed as 30 players fighting for one cause, and that was to really help us win the series."

Steve Smith may not have been as influential but he too contributed to the unbeaten run enjoyed by the team that evolved as the midweek side.

"He was strong, tough and didn't hold back when the going got rough," recalled Evans. "You could say he was a players player, no different to Donal on the pitch but very different off it.

"He won the drinking - by a mile. You never heard Stevie Smith say much until he had a couple of pints. Then you couldn't bloody well shut him up. It wasn't until about eight or nine o'clock at night when he had a dozen or so pints that he came into his own!"

Jones takes up the story: "We didn't really know him until a couple of weeks into the tour. I know these were amateur days, but we worked very hard in the early stages of the tour to devise a pattern of play and we treated it very, very seriously.

"But as in all tours, there comes a time when it is essential to get to know the guys around you better. You need this kind of bonding and invariably it means getting together for a couple, and a couple of more drinks. You don't bond with guys just on a rugby pitch. You do it socially.

"If we had gone out there to focus solely on rugby, nobody would ever probably have got to know Stevie Smith because he never talked much. But when we went out socially, sat down and had a few pints, it didn't take long to get to know him ... and very well at that.

"He was a top man to have in your corner unless you were in a round with him. You wouldn't have wanted him in your corner then. It wasn't that he was reluctant to buy, but more the fact that he was capable of putting us all away to bed.

"One of phrases used by Donal Lenihan was - cometh the hour, cometh the man - and that applied to Stevie on social occasions almost as much as it reflected his absolute dedication on the field of play. He was a wonderful tourist and a great addition to the party.

"You must remember, we knew all about Donal's exploits on the pitch. We knew he was a seasoned tourist and we appreciated his sense of humour as well. We knew all about Brendan Mullin, the shining light of Irish rugby for a few years before. We didn't know anything about Stevie Smith but it didn't take us long to find out!

"The Irish players on that tour helped bring everyone together. Of course, you want the best players you can get but you don't just want rugby players alone. You also need people with personality. Lions tours are all about mixing people from four different countries as quickly as possible and it is a difficult task by its very nature

"Apart from the contributions on the pitch, and that was immense, the Irish did a huge job in helping that process become a reality. I think it is just in the nature of the Irish people to be able to do that. Becoming close off the field helps to find a successful formula on it."

The important thing, according to Evans, is that on a Lions tour there can be no place for cliques. "You cannot have any doubts about fellow players when you are 10,000 miles away from home and you have to get through it on your own steam. Any sign of developments like that and the Irish soon put a stop to it."

155

1989 RESULTS

Played	Won	Drew	Lost	For	Against
12	11	0	1	360	182

Western Australia	W	44-0
Australia B	W	23-8
Queensland	W	19-12
Queensland B	W	30-6
New South Wales	W	23-21
New South Wales B	W	39-19
AUSTRALIA	L	12-30
ACT	W	41-25
AUSTRALIA	W	19-12
AUSTRALIA	W	19-18
NSW Country	W	72-13
ANZAC	W	19-15

Midweek captain Donal Lenihan leads the Lions out to face another battle

Paul Dean made just one appearance before injury wrecked his tour

Stevie Smith was the "Quiet Man" of the 1989 tour until .....

Brendan Mullin makes two of his customary breaks during the 1989 tour

CHAPTER 11

A SHORT COLD WINTER

AFTER the high of beating Australia in 1989 came the low of losing yet another series to New Zealand. It was very much a case of the same old story - a little bit of bad luck here, a couple of crucially bad refereeing decisions and the plot was lost.

New Zealand won the first and third Tests and were considerably lucky in the opening match. Australian referee Brian Kinsey won no fans in the Lions camp when he awarded a late, late and much disputed penalty to allow the All Blacks take the match 20-18.

Unlike 1983, when defeat in the first game saw things go from bad to worse, this Gavin Hastings led side picked themselves up, dusted themselves down and won their first match against New Zealand since the second of four Tests back in 1977.

That, however, was not good enough. The All Blacks came storming back in the third and won it easily to secure another overall victory against the touring side.

In relation to Ciaran Fitzgerald's 1983 Lions, this was probably less successful. Sure, Fitzgerald's men were beaten in each and every match by the All Blacks and also lost to Auckland and Canterbury.

The difference was that, apart from the last Test, they were never embarrassed on the field of play.

The 1993 Lions were. From the moment they lost the fifth game against Otago the morale of the players appeared to go downhill.

Hastings did everything he could to keep the show on the road but it was clear that many of the players who hadn't made the Test side were already thinking of the journey home by the mid point of the tour.

Successive defeats by Auckland and Hawkes Bay in between the first and second Tests and another by Waikato before the third merely emphasised the point that many players had lost confidence in the management and interest in playing for the good of the squad.

Welsh scrum half Robert Jones, an ever present on the Lions Test side in Australia four years earlier, didn't make the cut on this occasion but still felt honoured at being chosen on a tour for the second time.

However, he pointed out there were major differences between the thinking of players in 1989 and 1993.

"There were absolutely no rifts between the players in 1989 and I realised that even though I was in the Test side. In 1993, from a very early point, there was a clear understanding there was a clear divide between the guys in the midweek team and the people in the Test side.

"I don't think the manager, Geoff Cooke, was quite able to handle the situation that arose. From the week before the first Test, right the way through, there was even a split in training. We stayed with the assistant coach Dick Best and did our own thing.

"We got on with Best and waited for the first team to finish. That was ridiculous when you consider that a number of players, myself included, were going to sit on the bench for the first big game but had no role to play in the build up to the match.

"I know the situation that existed was not the only reason why we lost the series but it did play a significant part. When players are not allowed to express themselves and to be competitive in an attempt to prove they are as good or better than the next guy, then you really don't have much at all. I think too many people realised from a very early stage that they weren't going to be part of it.

"There were players on that tour who had performed very well in the Five Nations Championship, people who must have had a chance of selection for the Tests. It appeared the management had pre-conceived notions about who was going to play in those games and the others were just not given a chance to prove themselves. That was sad from every point of view. There was nobody there to take a guy aside and encourage him to give it a go. Players just felt they weren't wanted and they reacted as most people would - by just giving up on it.

"It's difficult to motivate yourself day in and day out if you know you haven't got a chance at the end of the day anyway."

That's not to say that players were unable to amuse themselves in the midst of all this strife. As usual, the Irish were central figures in the entertainment stakes.

Ireland had only two players originally selected on that touring party - Nick Popplewell and Mick Galwey - although the representation swelled to four eventually when Richard Wallace and Vinny Cunningham were flown out as replacements.

Popplewell was an ever present on the Test side, the only one of the four to clinch a place, but he was also very active off the field.

Affectionately known as Poppy, he installed himself as "Judge" for the many court sessions held during the eight weeks of the tour.

Ieuan Evans laughed as he recalled Popplewell's way of doing business: "He was a pretty brutal judge, more like the hanging judge. If you had to stand in front of him and he had a hard day physically, the black cap came on automatically. He was deadpan in his delivery, his put-down lines were excellent but thankfully this wasn't quite real life!

"On a more serious note, Poppy was a superb player. He had a great Test series. Nobody got the better of him on the pitch and nobody really got the better of him off it either."

When Ireland met England at Lansdowne Road on March 20 1993, it should have come as no surprise that they were quoted at long odds with the bookmakers.

England had strung together six victories in a row and had absolutely hammered Ireland in three of those games.

The previous year at Twickenham was an embarrassment as England scorched to a 38-9 victory.

Will Carling and his men were favourites to return to England after securing another easy win.

It was not to be. Ireland produced a huge performance and led 12-3 going into the final stages of the game.

By then, England were down and very much out. When Ireland moved into an attacking position near the end of the game, Mick Galwey emerged from a rolling maul and crashed over in the corner with two English defenders, one of them Rory Underwood, desperately hanging off him. The try probably secured his place on the Lions tour although he was brought as a flanker and not a second row.

That score line may also have been significant in Will Carling losing out as captain of the touring party and, given the way he lost interest in the proceedings after being dropped following the first Test, it was probably just as well.

In support of the theory that Messrs Cooke, Best and coach Ian McGeechan did not combine successfully to bring the best out of this particular touring party, I remember Galwey speaking to me in frustration early on the trip. In the middle of a training session, Best is alleged to have suggested to him that he had virtually no chance of making the Test side.

It was the type of attitude adapted towards many others as the tour progressed and may even have been levelled at England's golden boy Carling, although to his credit the English captain never gave less than his best as many of the midweek team rolled over.

Robert Jones felt sorry for Galwey on that tour. "There is no doubt about it, Mick Galwey was a very good player and a very good tourist as well. Without him, that 1993 tour would have been a much duller experience.

"I get back to a point I always make. Players must be allowed compete for places. If they are not given that opportunity then there isn't much point of having a squad of 30 players.

"I'm sure Mick, like myself and others, was bitterly disappointed at not being given the chance, and you can only ask to be given the chance. If you are, and don't take it, that's fine. But if you're not, then that's a different matter altogether."

Jones roomed with Galwey on a couple of occasions and refused point blank to reveal any intimate stories of the capers they got up to. "Seriously, we had some great laughs and the one thing I will say about Mick Galwey is that he is one of the best organisers of drinks parties in the business.

"I you should always have a fair few Irish players in any Lions party because they're the only ones who can organise free booze in any number of pubs throughout the southern hemisphere!"

Showing an obvious affection for Galwey, Jones said: "I don't know what I can say about him, except that he is the same guy now that he was eight years ago. He was a good player then, he is a great player now and has the personality to go with it.

"It's difficult to pull out stories about the Irish because there were so many. What I will say is that they were always with us Welsh boys - and the first thing Mick did whenever they got into the various towns was to seek out an Irish pub and organise a free tab for the boys when required. You could say he was entertainments manager.

164

"The serious aspect of that, of course, is that it helps pull the players together. It's getting people to go out socially as a unit and, in ways, he probably did more than a lot of others to get the group together as one.

"That has all changed now that the game has gone professional, but a good night out on the town is an excellent way of bonding the players together as one. In 1993, we had a lot more than one good night out. Sweet memories!"

Neither Wallace or Cunningham made the cut either but Jason Leonard, the English prop who broke into the Test side for the second and third games against the All Blacks, had an opportunity to mix with both.

"I can't quite remember how many matches they each played but they were up there trying in the midweek side when others weren't.

"I don't quite know how Vinny managed to do it because he was out most of the time. Because he came out on the tour quite late, he was mostly on an extended holiday and he took full advantage of it.

"Funny thing is, the weather in New Zealand isn't great around that time of the year. Yet, Vinny walked around most of the day wearing sunglasses. I think it was because he was out that much he didn't want to give the game away by letting people see his eyes. He would have worn them to training had he been allowed."

Leonard once shared a room with Wallace and told a story against himself. "Richard was a really nice guy but a bit on the quiet side and he usually went to bed fairly early.

"He might have wished he hadn't on one particular night when I went out with some of the boys for a few drinks which turned into a bit of a session. I must have got one bad pint or something, but anyway I got back to the room and threw up.

"It wasn't your normal puke. It was everywhere, on my bed, on Richard's bed, in his kit back, on the carpet and in the bathroom. So I get up in the morning, get the terrible smell and sur-veyed the devastation. I knew I was in trouble so I decided to turn the blame back on Richard.

"I opened the door and one of the guys passing asked 'what's that smell?' I immediately told him that Richard had been very sick in the middle of the night, that he couldn't hold his drink and that the 'crime' should be punished in our court.

"I nipped down to breakfast and Richard woke up in the meantime. He followed me down and immediately accused me of throwing up but I had told all the boys that he had done it. Nobody believed him and I was off the hook – at least for a few days. We had a good laugh at his expense during that time."

1993 RESULTS

Played	Won	Drew	Lost	For	Against
13	7	0	6	314	285

North Auckland	W	30-17
North Harbour	W	29-13
New Zealand Maoris	W	24-20
Canterbury	W	28-10
Otago	L	24-37
Southland	W	34-16
NEW ZEALAND	L	18-20
Taranaki	W	49-25
Auckland	L	18-23
Hawkes Bay	L	17-29
NEW ZEALAND	W	20-7
Waikato	L	10-38
NEW ZEALAND	L	13-30

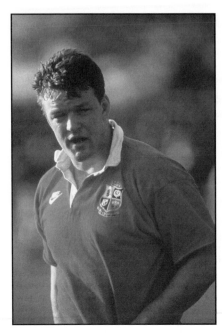

Mick Galwey in his first Lions appearance in 1993

Head down, Galwey bursts through

Two faces, much the same face, of Nick Popplewell, the "honorary" Irishman in the 1993 Lions Test pack

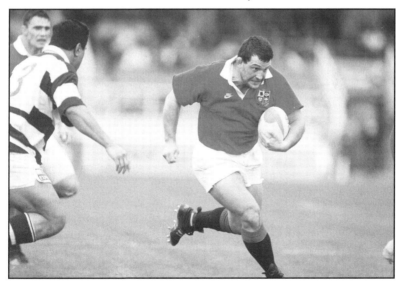

Vinny Cunningham – without the shades!.

Richard Wallace, the first of three brothers to make the Lions squad

CHAPTER 12

THE LIONS ROAR AGAIN

THE 1997 Lions were the first professionals to undertake a tour and the first to take on the reigning World Champions.

The World Cup was won in 1987 by New Zealand and in 1991 by Australia so that by the time the Lions went to play the All Blacks in 1993, their neighbours had dethroned the inaugural winners.

Francois Pienaar and Nelson Mandela held the William Webb Ellis trophy aloft together after a controversial final victory over New Zealand in 1995. Now, the remaining ambition of the Springboks was to confirm their status with a series victory over the Lions.

It was not to be and the Lions returned home in triumph after an amazing victory, despite the fact that they lost the final Test.

It didn't matter that England provided what appeared to be an unbalanced section of the party - no less than 18 of the 35 players. It didn't matter that the Lions had to dig deep. This was a happy tour, a contented group that benefited from an influential group of just four Irishmen.

Ieuan Evans, in his last Lions tour, recalls the trip with fond memories. The Lions themselves captured many off field moments on video and one of the highlights was the head-bashing, blue language, pep talk given by Irish hooker Keith Wood before the first Test.

Even though England's Martin Johnson was the tour captain and had his own influential style, Wood was certainly more vociferous in his bid to whip up enthusiasm.

"Those who watched the video will probably remember more about the tour than I do in that sense. But yes, it does tell part of the story about the tour. When you go to South Africa to play rugby you are really stepping onto a different planet. They are intense about the game. Rugby is surely a religion.

"The only way we were going to beat them was to upset them. We took the game to them and did it through terrific self-belief in the face of adversity. Keith Wood was a star man in that respect.

"Eric Miller was unlucky not to play through the Test series but was always pushing. He was terrific, a great athletic talent but he found it impossible to get into the side once we won the first Test.

"The bulk of the squads in the last three tours has been from England, but I always get back to the point that success comes about when there is real competition for places.

"Not many people would have thought that all four Irishmen would have been pushing for places in the Test side in 1997 and that three of them actually made it.

But Keith Wood, Paul Wallace and Jeremy Davidson were all worthy of their places and Eric would have been at ease in that team as well.

"A lot of the great performances came from the group outside the England camp."

Even English player Jason Leonard agreed with that assessment.

"I've been on three Lions tours, and on each occasion it's remarkable that there was one of the Wallace brothers on the trips.

"In 1993 it was Richard, 1997 Paul and 2001 David. One of the things I cannot do is refer to David as 'Wally' because to me there is only one man with that nickname and that's Paul.

"Even though 1997 was a professional tour, Wally still managed to cram in a lot of enjoyment to go with the hard work. He will probably kill me for saying it, but I'm going to anyway because I think it should be a matter for the record.

"He was the only one, if there was a night out in 1997, to be able to go out for a drink with the lads and be the last one left in the bar but the first one up for training the following day. I'm sure he trained as many times half gone than he did when sober. Sorry Wally, but it's bloody true!"

"On the pitch, Wally was equally amazing. I mean, nobody gave him much chance of getting in the Test side but he gave it everything from the word go. The South Africans reckoned they would murder him in the scrums, but after the first in the opening Test he never had a problem. I thought he had a magnificent tour and played a huge role in the victories over South Africa.

"It was much the same for Jeremy Davidson. He wasn't tipped by too many to get a crack at a Test place but worked extremely hard as well. The thing about these two that was amazing is that they also played hard socially but still managed to push out the boat at training. I reckon the coaching staff didn't cop a thing although both Wally and Jeremy must have been suffering inside. That's the thing about younger guys; they can go out and enjoy themselves but recover quickly. At my age, I'm not capable of doing that any more."

Miller would certainly have made the cut for the Test side were it not for an illness that struck before the first big match.

Leonard believes Miller made huge strides during that tour and recounts a story at the very beginning to back up that claim. "At the start of the tour, people were tested for body fat. There was nothing much in it except to see what state the guys were in and whether anything could be done to reduce it. Eric, despite his slim

174

looking build, was the fattest member of the touring party at about 20 odd per cent.

"To look at him, he's a natural athlete but he had this body fat and got absolutely paranoid about it. Every time he passed a mirror he would look at himself, pinch himself, roll the fat between his fingers and turn sideways. I think for the first four days after that he only ate fruit. We gave him a bit of stick about it, took food away from him and then put mounds of food in front of him to tempt him at different stages.

"The hard training and self-determination worked for him though. By the end of the tour he was probably the skinniest one of the party. Then we started telling him he looked like Ali McBeal and he didn't quite like that either. Let's put it this way, we had a bit of fun with him!"

The star of the series was Keith Wood. Remembered with affection by Leonard, the English player described him as "awesome."

"It's hard for me to say who contributed most to the success of the tour because many individuals played their part in different ways. Jeremy Guscott won the series with his drop goal in the second Test but, if I was pushed, I would have to say that Woodie was the most consistent player of the lot."

Wood had major injury problems in the months leading up to the tour but made it and then got in the Test team despite various other niggling injuries picked up in South Africa.

It was just what Wood wanted and just what the Lions needed.

From the early stages of the tour, Wood established himself as Martin Johnson's right hand man, the vociferous one against Johnson's determined but calmer approach to match days.

He remembers that first scrum when the Lions were shoved a yard and ended up in a crumpled heap. He remembers the pack didn't get the timing right and remembers watching the bulky South African pack buckle with tiredness as the minutes ticked by.

175

The South Africans will forever describe the first Test victory as grand larceny or as close as damned to it.

Wood prefers to remember it as one of the great comebacks when the Lions scored late tries by Matt Dawson and Alan Tait to win the game 25-16. "It's an 80 minute game and you have to play to the end."

The circumstances were similar in the crucial second game. The Lions conceded three tries but won 18-15 thanks to Neil Jenkins, Guscott and Wood. Jenkins knocked over five penalties and Guscott got the winning drop goal but Wood put the Lions in the position to score in the first place.

Having survived tremendous Springbok pressure, he broke down the narrow side and kicked down the touchline to force South Africa concede the throw. From there, Guscott found the space to kick the winning points.

He had to wait a bit longer to actually see the moment of glory because, when Guscott dropped the goal, Wood was buried under a pile of bodies in a ruck. The game was also his swansong on the 1997 tour. Later in the game he tackled South African Fritz van Heerden and tore his groin. When the celebrations began on the pitch, Wood was in agony … but also in ecstasy drooling at the thought of what he and his team had achieved.

The Irish hooker played no part in the third Test. The week was spent reflecting on seven glorious weeks, and the world of rugby had time to reflect on the stunning contribution made by one Keith Gerard Mallinson Wood.

1997 RESULTS

Played	Won	Drew	Lost	For	Against
13	11	0	2	480	278

Eastern Province	W	25-16
Border	W	18-14
Western Province	W	38-21
Mpumalanga	W	64-14
Northern Transvaal	L	30-35
Gauteng	W	20-14
Natal	W	42-12
Emerging Springboks	W	51-22
SOUTH AFRICA	W	25-16
Free State	W	52-30
SOUTH AFRICA	W	18-15
Northern Free State	W	67-39
SOUTH AFRICA	L	16-35

Keith Wood in action against Natal

Eric Miller in flying form.

Paul Wallace in the driving seat.

Jeremy Davidson reaches for the sky.

The fighting Irishmen of 1997.

CHAPTER 13

IRELAND MARCH ON

The background to selection of the Lions party to tour Australia was one of frustration from an Irish point of view.

The 1999/2000 season started in dismal fashion in Twickenham but when coach Warren Gatland rang the changes for the match with Scotland at Lansdowne Road, there was a remarkable upturn in fortunes.

Ireland won three out of their four remaining matches that season before embarking on a mildly successful tour of Argentina, the USA and Canada.

In the autumn of 2000, Ireland smashed Japan into submission and were then horribly unlucky to have lost to South Africa at Lansdowne Road.

With those friendlies behind them, the Irish faced into the Six Nations Championship and, with a spring in their steps, accounted for Italy in Rome and then France at Lansdowne Road.

Although the 22-15 win was clouded in controversy because of a controversial try scored by Brian O'Driscoll, the way looked clear for Ireland to finish high up in the Championship. Dare I say it, there was even talk about winning the Grand Slam!

The rampant outbreak of Foot and Mouth disease in Britain and to a much more limited extent in Ireland put an end to Ireland's gallop, however, and all three remaining games – against Wales, Scotland and England were deferred to the Autumn.

Undoubtedly, those postponements had a major bearing on the selection process for the trip to Australia, and adversely affected at least two or three Irish players vying for positions in the 37 strong squad.

Peter Clohessy was probably the most frustrated and disappointed at his failure to make it.

Back in 1997, Clohessy was an original selection but had to withdraw because of a back injury. Paul Wallace was called up and he went on to establish a place in the Test side against the South Africans.

Clohessy, although pushing on in terms of age, was probably in the best physical condition he had ever been. He set his sights on the tour many months before and enjoyed a brilliant season for Munster, whom he helped guide into the Heineken European Cup semi-finals, and Ireland.

Sympathy for Munster and Irish colleague John Hayes was tempered by the fact that he will still probably be around to push for selection in four years time. This was Clohessy's last stand and it didn't help that, instead of injuries to props, all the front row injury problems on this Lions tour affected hookers so there was no chance of him being called up.

Denis Hickie was another unlucky Irishman. He broke his hand in December of 2000 and then the Foot and Mouth shutdown added to his problems. He played barely half a dozen games in six months and that must have counted against him.

Ireland, therefore, had six players named in the original party although that swelled to eight with the arrival of Tyrone Howe and David Wallace as replacements during the tour.

The Irish "bankers" were Keith Wood, Brian O'Driscoll and Malcolm O'Kelly in that order, but happily the representation was not confined to that trio. Ronan O'Gara and Rob Henderson who made their mark on the Six Nations games and Jeremy Davidson, whose experience from 1997 helped his case considerably, were also chosen.

England, the dominant force in European rugby over a number of seasons, had 18 representatives on the squad, Wales ten, Ireland six and Scotland three.

Inevitably, the breakdown prompted discussion and argument. Very few could deny the English their place in the sun on the basis of previous form, but there were some eyebrows raised at the Welsh being nominated for ten places.

The influence of coach Graham Henry (the devils you know are better than the devils you don't know) is likely to have been a major factor in that.

Certainly, the selection of the entire Welsh front and back rows appeared to be a bit much particularly with Clohessy and Wallace screaming for recognition.

Not everyone agrees with the views of former Irish international second row Neil Francis but he put his finger on the pulse when he suggested in his weekly Sunday Tribune column: "It was the worst case of ten guineas for the piebald, boss.

"It was also 1-0 to Henry in terms of whom will become in the dominant partner in the Lions' management axis." How right he was.

O'Driscoll's selection was greeted enthusiastically, as expected, by all sections of the media, Irish, English, Welsh and Scottish. There was never a doubt, never a murmur of protest against a young man who did everything possible to turn the Test series in favour of the Lions.

He played in six games on tour including the three Tests. He was a key figure in all of them but most especially in the opening match against the Wallabies in Brisbane.

The international rugby arena is liberally sprinkled with examples of great scores. Videos have been produced of the best tries and, in the past, thousands of rugby supporters have their own special memories of scores and of matches, many of them involving the Lions.

I remember seeing a film clip of former Irish and Lions out half Jackie Kyle scoring a try against Wales in the late 1940's. I can't pinpoint the actual game but I could describe the try in detail over and over again.

The try scored by Gareth Edwards in that magnificent match between the Barbarians and New Zealand in Cardiff in 1973 is another that won't be forgotten.

Neither is one by Ollie Campbell against Waikato in the penultimate game of the 1983 Lions tour to New Zealand.

Up to 2001, that was the best individual try I ever had the pleasure to see. Campbell, if my memory serves me well, beat eight players and a few of them twice as he weaved his way through the defence before crashing over in the corner.

Waikato folk are partisan when it comes to rugby, but even they were moved to give Campbell a standing ovation. I would love to see it again on screen but have to content myself with playing it over and over again in my mind.

Things move on. Records are there to be broken and I now believe O'Driscoll emulated Campbell with his try in the first Test at the Gabba.

This was a classic individual try against a team that prided itself in having the tightest and meanest defence in world rugby. O'Driscoll smashed his way through the initial gap and then took off on a fantastic run to leave several first-line defenders and Australian full back Matt Burke in an embarrassed heap on the ground. Allowing for the Test series loss, that try is being and will be talked about for decades to come.

O'Kelly, Davidson and O'Gara failed to make the Test side. O'Kelly, in particular, will be disappointed because he didn't seize the opportunity early in the tour. Davidson also had to be happy with appearances in the less important games along with O'Gara, but none of them lost sight of the importance of their roles on tour.

O'Gara, in particular, was pushed from pillar to post and virtually ignored by coach Henry, but kept his dignity and vowed to use the experience for personal improvement purposes.

"No matter what happened on tour, I think it was a great experience. I realise there are certain things I want to do to make myself a better player and I will set out to achieve that when I get back to Ireland," he said.

Wood came into the tour in pole position to take the number two shirt. Perhaps the greatest threat to that ambition may have been England's Phil Greening, but we will never know because Greening was injured so early on.

There was never a debate after that. Robin McBryde and Gordon Bulloch were never in the same class and Dorian West, another replacement, had no time to make up lost ground.

In any event, Wood made a spectacular contribution to the Lions' bid for victory and even had the audacity of attempting to rub salt into the Wallaby wounds in the first Test with a long-range drop goal attempt.

There was never any doubt about his commitment, his determination and his sheer skill and power, credentials that have helped give him the reputation of being the best hooker in world rugby.

Rob Henderson was looked upon as a "wild card" candidate for selection in the party of 37 and an outsider for the Test team.

He surprised everyone except perhaps the Lions management. Henderson had made spectacular progress from the time he engaged a personal trainer just a year before. He was stronger, fitter and wiser and was blindly determined not to allow this unique opportunity pass him by.

Sure, he had a bit of luck on his side. Will Greenwood was injured against New South Wales and ruled out of the first Test. In fact, Greenwood didn't play again on tour, but it is very doubtful whether he could have pushed Henderson out based on the display he produced in that memorable game at the Gabba.

Blistering runs, one of them leading to the Lions fourth try by Scott Quinnell, and smashing tackles were the hallmarks of Henderson's game that evening. His display in that match vindicated the decision to select him and, even if circumstances didn't allow for the same type of quality performances in the last two games, Henderson made a stunning contribution to the tour of 2001.

Although most Irish fans were clamouring to have Hickie chosen when Dan Luger's injury denied the Lions of a Test winger, I believed it unfair when some made a harsh judgement on Howe's call-up.

He is a classic example of a player who put hard times behind him to emerge onto the international stage and make his mark at that level.

Howe had suffered a serious injury that kept him out of the game for nearly three years. At one stage, he believed he would never play again but he made a remarkable recovery before making a late charge for glory.

In six international appearances for Ireland, Howe scored three tries and proved himself equally good at defending. These were qualities that endeared him to the Lions selectors and particularly to Scottish representative John Rutherford, a Lions player in 1983 and 1986.

Early in the tour I had the opportunity to speak to Rutherford and Howe's name came up when discussing the list of players on the stand-by list.

"More than one of us was impressed by Tyrone Howe. I think he is a very high quality footballer with rounded skills and he doesn't make many mistakes. Denis Hickie would have been high on our priorities but he was injured quite a lot. Howe is also a very good finisher and that's why he came so much into the reckoning."

The arrival of Wallace undoubtedly sparked off a celebration in the family home. He followed the footsteps of brothers Richard (1993 to New Zealand) and Paul (1997 to South Africa) and the family now hold the unique record of being the only three brothers to have made Lions tours.

It was too late for him to make the impact he desired but he played exceptionally well in his only full game against ACT and has time on his side to make a second tour to New Zealand in 2005.

Old Friends Peter Clohessy and Mick Galwey line out for Ireland. Galwey made it to New Zealand in 1993 but Clohessy missed out twice for Lions selection. Picked in 1997 he withdrew before the tour with injury and then was a surprise omission for the tour to Australia in 2001.

The eight Irishmen in jovial mood

CHAPTER 14

THE START OF AN ADVENTURE

EASTERN Australians regard Perth as a place "somewhere over there." It is a well-designed and well-ordered city built on the banks of the Swan River.

Rugby is not that well supported and few of the top players reside there. It is an area populated by a lot of New Zealanders and other nationalities. In the past and indeed this year, the Western Australia side was comprised of an enthusiastic group of amateur players.

For all of Perth's apparent isolation, it is a very pleasant city with a very agreeable climate (even if the weather for the game was unusually cold) and every effort was made to make the Lions stay in Fremantle as pleasant as possible.

Lions manager Donal Lenihan hand-picked the Esplanade Hotel and the resort to allow the squad relax and unwind in relatively peaceful surroundings for the first week of the tour. He and the players knew there would be no pressure in this particular game. The pressure only began when the squad moved east to where the real interest in Australian rugby lies.

In that sense, for all major visiting rugby teams, Perth is really only a stop-off point.

Match 1: Western Australia
WACA Ground, Perth, June 8.
Attendance: 20,695. Weather: Cool, damp. Pitch: Soft.

WESTERN AUSTRALIA 10 (B. Becroft, R. Barugh try each)
BRITISH AND IRISH LIONS 116 (D. Luger, S. Quinnell 3 tries
each, R. Howley, N. Back, I. Balshaw 2 tries each, W. Greenwood,
M. Taylor, S. Taylor, A. Healey, B. O'Driscoll, D. Grewcock 1 try
each, R. O'Gara 13 conversions)

IT would be fair to say that the Lions probably broke more
sweat in any of their training sessions up to this than they did at
the WACA Ground in Perth against a woefully inept Western
Australia side.

It was aptly described as a total mis-match by former
Australian skipper Nick Farr-Jones who warned the Lions not to
read much into this astonishingly one sided game.

Records tumbled as they ripped Western Australia apart from
the outset. They overtook the previous high score of 97-0, created
in South Africa 25 years ago, and rattled up the biggest Lions scoring total and winning margin in history.

Farr-Jones remarked: "This was a professional team in action
against an amateur one and a poor amateur side as well. You wonder whether it did them any good at all, but I suppose they had to
get a match under their belt.

"They played some stunning rugby and scored some great
tries but they would be wise to put it to the back of their minds.
They have much tougher games ahead and won't be given anything like the same room in those."

Happily, the warning appears to have been taken seriously by
the Lions. Coach Graham Henry noted: "We won't have it as easy
again and on a scale of one to ten, taking into account the opposition, I would give the side six for that performance.

"We still have a huge amount of work to do. We lost a bit of our structure at times and we have got to ensure individuals play a little more unselfishly.

"We will get to work on analysis of the performance and I'm sure we will find many things we can improve on. But when you score 116 points and 18 tries in any game, you have got to be happy too.

"The main aim of this tour is to play good rugby and win all our games. We have started with a positive performance in general, and I think you have to give the guys credit for scoring all those tries.

"It is going to be much more difficult from the next game on. The Queensland President's XV will have a number of Super 12 players in their side and we will have to move up a gear to take them on.

"After that, it is going to get tougher and tougher and the next four weeks will tell a lot more about the quality of this side than this."

For the Irish, it was a good day with all four of the starting side playing influential roles in the victory.

Ronan O'Gara kicked 26 points and helped create a number of tries as the Lions cut loose.

The jury was still out afterwards on Brian O'Driscoll as a full back but he played reasonably well before reverting to centre in the last quarter. There, he made his mark by scoring the last of the 18 tries.

Keith Wood captained the side and produced a typically vigorous display that also won him praise from Henry.

Arguably, however, Malcolm O'Kelly was the best of the four. He destroyed Western Australia out of touch and secured invaluable possession for his side at a number of the many re-starts the home side had to take. He also had a superb display in the loose and even managed a beautiful left footed punt to create one of the early Lions tries. It all prompted Henry to remark: "He had a pretty flawless game."

The Man of the Match award, however, went to Scott Quinnell based on his powerful play and the hat trick of tries he scored. Quinnell often decimated the Western Australian defence and, even against this lowly opposition, made an immediate claim for a place in the Test side.

Dan Luger was another who appeared back to his best and became the second player to score three times, while Will Greenwood and Rob Howley were others in the Lions back division to impress.

Western Australia captain Trefor Thomas was full of praise for the Lions. "We set ourselves some goals. One of them was to score at least two tries and we did that. Unfortunately, because of the strength of the opposition, we were unable to achieve any of the others. They were very impressive. They are a very strong side and a very creative one. I think they will go well on this tour."

Inevitably however, the home players were as embarrassed as they were disappointed. "We could have done without a hiding like this," said Thomas.

The WACA ground is normally reserved for cricket and one Australian official wondered aloud whether that was the fastest century ever seen there. Even the dejected Thomas managed a smile at that!

The Lions set out their stall as early as the second minute when Quinnell went over for the opening try. The home fans booed but were quickly silenced when Rob Howley went in for a second score in the eighth minute. 14-0 to the Lions and there was only going to be one outcome.

The British and Irish press corps threw in five dollars a man before the game to a sweep fund to predict the winning margin. I gave the Lions a 43-point start but they hit that mark within 36 minutes. By half time they were 57 points to the good.

Another nine in the second followed nine tries in the first half and the only saving grace for Western Australia was that they scored twice.

Still, for all their enthusiasm and Austin Healey's 76th minute try brought the Lions total beyond the 100 mark for the first time in their history.

After O'Driscoll's 78th minute try to push the score out to 116, referee Wayne Erickson decided against playing any stoppage time and wisely called a halt to the proceedings.

It all begged the question – did it do anyone any good?

Well, some say it was a farce of a match and it was. But former Wallaby skipper Andrew Slack begged to differ.

Slack did make the comment: "It was a little bit odd that the game played was rugby and not cricket. The WACA scoreboard hadn't had the numbers rolling over so quickly since Barry Richards scored 325 in a day during a Sheffield Shield cricket match 30 years ago."

He added: The first ever professional Lions team to visit Australia began their tour against a bunch of amateurs, many of whom might struggle to hold down regular first grade spots in any club side on the east coast of Australia.

"Genuine superstars of a multi-million dollar sporting enterprise were pitched against anonymous, and for the most part, moderately talented enthusiasts. It was like Tiger Woods taking on a 12-handicapper."

The suggestion afterwards was that Western Australia should have imported some guest players for the occasion. Slack disagreed. "I don't think that would have achieved much. Had the home side been stacked with blow-ins from other states, and the margin of loss reduced to 40 or 50 points, any satisfaction derived by the locals in playing for their state would have been severely diluted.

"The Western Australian team know they're not a world power in the game, but it shouldn't reduce the pride with which

196

they play for the state. If the majority of players were called in from elsewhere for the few times they had a big fixture, the whole purpose of the exercise would be defeated.

"The Lions could not categorise this fixture as appropriate preparation for the Test series, but in reality there were only a couple of things they needed to achieve.

"The first was to ensure there were no significant injuries and the second was to finally get on the field and blow off some cobwebs after a lengthy period of training without games.

"Outside of the Wallaby management, spectators received value for money. For those with no need of putting together tactical briefs, there was plenty to enjoy.

"Some of the world's best players demonstrated their skills and the local Davids whacked Goliath right between the eyes on a couple of occasions, even if the giant was always in control. It was all a bit of fun and I see nothing wrong with that. Sometimes in rugby we can take ourselves all too seriously."

SCORING SEQUENCE
FIRST HALF

2 mins - Scott Quinnell try, R.O'Gara conversion. 7-0.

8 mins - Rob Howley try, O'Gara conversion. 14-0.

14 mins - Dan Luger try. 19-0

17 mins - Will Greenwood try. 24-0.

27 mins - Neil Back try, O'Gara conversion. 31-0.

30 mins - Neil Back try. 36-0.

36 mins - Danny Grewcock try. O'Gara conversion. 43-0.

38 mins - S.cott Quinnell try, O'Gara conversion. 50-0.

40 mins - Dan Luger try, O'Gara conversion. 57-0.

SECOND HALF

5 MINS - Rob Howley try 62.0. O'Gara conversion. 64-0

9 mins - Mark Taylor try. 69-0.

12 mins - Brian Becdroft try 69-5.

18 mins - Simon Taylor try. O'Gara conversion. 76-5

23 mins - Dan Luger try, O'Gara conversion. 83-5.

29 mins - Rob Barugh try. 83-10.

31 mins - Iain Balshaw try, O'Gara conversion. 90-10.

35 mins - Scott Quinnell try, O'Gara conversion. 97-10

36 mins - Austin Healey try, O'Gara conversion. 104-10.

37 mins - Iain Balshaw try, O'Gara conversion. 111-10.

39 mins - Brian O'Driscoll try. 116-10.

WESTERN AUSTRALIA: S. Apaapa, M. Gardiner, A. Broughton, H. Waldin, B. Becroft, T. Feather, M. Fleet, T. Stevens, C. Duff, A. New, N. Hollis, T. Thomas captain; H. Grace, A. Brain, R. Coney.

Replacements. D. McRae for Feather (22), R. Barugh for Flett (52), M. Harrington for Waldin (66), R. Kellam for Duff (64), G. Plimmer for Coney (70)

THE LIONS: B. O'Driscoll (Ireland), B. Cohen (England), M. Taylor (Wales), W. Greenwood (England), D. Luger (England), R. O'Gara (Ireland), R. Howley (Wales), D. Morris (Wales), K. Wood (Ireland) captain; Pl. Vickery (England), D. Grewcock (England), M. O'Kelly (Ireland), R. Hill (England), S. Quinnell (Wales), N. Back (England).

Replacements. S. Taylor (Scotland) for Hill (injured 40), A. Healey (England) for Howley (55), I. Balshaw (England) for Greenwood (injured 58), J. Leonard (England) for Vickery (60), R. Henderson (Ireland) for Cohen (66), R. McBryde (Wales) for Wood, J. Davidson (Ireland) for Grewcock (both 73).

Referee. W. Erickson (Australia).

Lions record against Western Australia
1930: Lions 71 Western Australia 3
1966: Lions 60 Western Australia 3
1989: Lions 44 Western Australia 0
2001: Lions 116 Western Australia 10

CHAPTER 15

THE GREAT BARRIER REEF

PREDICTIONS that the Queensland Presidents XV would pose more problems for the Lions than Western Australia were right … and wrong.

While the records fell like wickets at the WACA in Perth, the Lions created their own bit of history second time around by scoring 73 points in the 40 minutes after half time.

It was calculated to impress and one had to pity Queensland coach Peter Grigg who was the butt of several jokes the following day on his return to Brisbane.

One joker, on board his aircraft on the way home, suggested that Grigg was retiring as a rugby coach and taking up a new post in cricket!

There was a happy outcome to the game as well as a most pleasant stay in Townsville. Blue skies, acceptably high temperatures and accessibility to the Great Barrier Reef made Townsville a very agreeable place.

Mind you, Ireland's Rob Henderson thought he might never make it. Henderson, at the best of times, does not like flying. He admits: "If I go on holiday, I prefer to cycle. I hate boats and planes particularly. If someone pushes the call bell to order a drink, I start to panic."

Manager Donal Lenihan went to great lengths to ensure that travel on this trip was kept to an absolute minimum. Most of the press and supporters travelled to Townsville from Perth via either Melbourne or Adelaide and Brisbane – three flights and 12 hours of travel.

Lenihan organised that the Lions would travel on a charter with just a re-fuelling stop off at Alice Springs.

The Lions set out for the airport at 10.am on the day following the match. They arrived at their destination 17 hours later!

After checking in for their flight, the plane was found to have developed a technical fault. A back up aircraft was provided but that too developed a fault.

The Lions were allowed leave the airport and headed back into Perth where they had lunch and some relaxation at the plush Burswood Resort and Casino.

Henderson and other whiled the time away by playing black-jack. For Henderson, it was too much time to think. For Jason Leonard it was too much time to play. He lost over $1000 dollars and reckoned the Lions management should have compensated him!

The end result was that the party didn't arrive in Townsville until three o'clock on Sunday morning and a planned training session for that day never materialised.

It mattered little to the outcome of the game. At one stage of the second half, Grigg contacted one of the back-room coaches through walkie-talkie and asked him to get the ground staff to switch off the lights.

Match 2: Queensland Presidents XV.
Dairy Farmers Stadium, Townsville, June 12
Attendance: 18,562. Weather: Warm. Pitch: Firm

QUEENSLAND PRESIDENTS XV 6 (S. Drahm 2 penalties) BRITISH AND IRISH LIONS 83 (J. Robinson 5 tries, R. Henderson 3 tries), C. Charvis 2 tries, D. Young, M. O'Kelly try each, penalty try, N. Jenkins 5 conversions, M. Perry 4 conversions).

JASON ROBINSON and Rob Henderson emerged as two of the main heroes as the British and Irish Lions smashed their way to another convincing victory.

The home fans in a crowd of 18,500 gasped in wonder as the deadly duo racked up eight of the Lions total of eleven tries in a 34 minute second half spell. The display prompted home coach Grigg to tip them for possible Test places. "Those two stood out amongst the rest of a very high quality back division that ran us ragged."

Robinson, the former Great Britain Rugby League star was the most lethal finisher on the pitch and grabbed an amazing five tries while Henderson, with a brilliant all-round distribution performance, scored a memorable hat trick.

The Lions played champagne rugby throughout that second half but neither Robinson or Henderson wished to take the credit.

"This was all about a team performance," said Robinson. "I'm a winger and I'm expected to finish off the chances when they come. A lot of the players inside made it very easy for me. We didn't really create much in the first 40 minutes and I got smashed a couple of times. But once the spaces opened up, all I really needed to do was finish the opportunities off.

"Hendo and Will Greenwood were magnificent out there. They made it look all so easy."

Henderson had to work a bit harder for his haul, particularly the first two. The Irish player put the Lions into a 34-6 lead with his 54th minute individual effort which involved a strong run, chip and chase which he described light heartedly as "originally an attempted drop kick."

"No, seriously, the guys outside me were calling it already to be put along the floor and I just happened to get there first. It was a nice feeling to score my first try for the Lions.

"It was even better to go on and score three and I would have to thank Matt Perry. He had Jason to his left and me to his right. I was screaming for the ball and I guess he felt, thankfully, that Jason had enough in five at that stage."

This was a very positive second half performance. From the Lions perspective, the first half was a shocker. They were unable to win quality possession out of touch, struggled to impose themselves in the scrums and the back line never moved with any degree of fluency.

When they did win good ball they proceeded to self-destruct. They took far too many risks from impossible positions and heaped mistake upon mistake.

The prime culprits were full back Perry and wings Robinson and Daffyd James. After the boost of two tries in the opening quarter, the Lions looked far from a top class international side.

In fact, the home side played most of the best rugby.

But that first half effort must have taken its toll because they never raised a challenge from the moment the Lions scored their third try 30 seconds into the second period - the signal for the floodgates to open.

From the opening seconds, when Man of the Match Colin Charvis scored the team's third try, it was a no contest situation.

Their scrummaging was more powerful and Gordon Bulloch, an early substitution for the injured Robin McBryde, found his targets out of touch. In that spell, Scott Murray and Jeremy Davidson cleaned Queensland out.

Starved of possession and run out of steam, the home side could only resort to desperate defence. But the Lions found the composure they lacked earlier and settled down to assess their play before taking full advantage.

The crowd loved it, particularly the large contingent from Britain and Ireland.

Their attendance and support so moved the Lions that the team came back on the pitch ten minutes after the finish to hail them.

"We were surprised that so many supporters should be there at this early stage of the tour and we really wanted to say thanks," said Henderson.

But in the late night pubs and clubs of Townsville, it was the fans that celebrated another significant Lions record-breaking achievement - 73 points in 40 minutes of rugby.

At that point of the itinerary, it was enough to suggest it could be a very good tour.

SCORING SEQUENCE
FIRST HALF

8 mins - Dai Young try. 5-0 to the Lions.

17 mins - Colin Charvis try. 10-0.

19 mins - Shane Drahm penalty. 10-3.

28 mins - S. Drahm penalty. 10-6.

SECOND HALF

30 secs - C. Charvis try, Neil Jenkins conversion. 17-6.

6 mins - Jason Robinson try. 22-6

10 mins - Penalty try, Jenkins conversion. 29-6

14 mins - Rob Henderson try, Jenkins conversion. 36-6

21 mins - J. Robinson try, Jenkins conversion. 43-6.

22 mins - R. Henderson try, Jenkins conversion. 50-6

26 mins - J. Robinson try. 55-6.

33 mins - Malcolm O'Kelly try, Matt Perry conversion. 62-6.

35 mins - J. Robinson try, Perry conversion. 69-6

38 mins - Robinson try, Perry conversion. 76-6

41 mins - Henderson try, Perry conversion. 83-6

QUEENSLAND PRESIDENTS XV: N. Williams, D. McCallum, J. Pelesasa, J. Ramsamy, S. Barton, S. Drahm, B. Wakely, R. Tyrell, S. Hardman Captain; F. Dyson, M. Mitchell, R. Vadelago, T. McVerry, J. Roe, S. Fava. Replacements. S. Kerr for Dyson (8). M. Tabrett for Williams (37), A. Scotney for Drahm (55), A. Farley for Hardman, T. Tavalea for Vedalago (both 63).

BRITISH AND IRISH LIONS: M. Perry (England), D. James (Wales), R. Henderson (Ireland), W. Greenwood (England), J. Robinson (England), N. Jenkins (Wales), M. Dawson (England), T. Smith (Scotland), R. McBryde (Wales), D. Young (Wales) Capain; J. Davidson (Ireland), S. Murray (Scotland), C. Charvis (Wales), M. Corry (England), M. Williams (Wales). Replacements. G. Bulloch

(Scotland) for McBryde (8), J. Leonard (England) for Smith (59), M. Taylor (Wales) for Greenwood, A. Healey (England) for Jenkins (both 63), M. O'Kelly (Ireland) for Davidson (67).

Referee. G. Ayoub (Sydney)

Lions Record against Queensland Presidents (Queensland B)
1989: Lions 30 Queensland B 6
2001: Lions 83 Queensland Presidents 6

CHAPTER 16

HEADY HEIGHTS

BRISBANE is a pretty city and blessed with a magnificent climate. Even during the short days of winter, the sun virtually always shines. Theirs is an outdoor culture, shorts, t-shirts and sandals.

To the north is the Sunshine Coast and to the South is the Gold Coast, the hub of which is Surfers Paradise.

A four day stay was all too short but the team, apart from the rigorous training regime set for them by coach Graham Henry, were able to pack in some sight-seeing, and a few hardy souls even went swimming with sharks.

Rob Henderson is noted for his bravery on the pitch but he's not quite the same man off it.

We learned early in the tour of his fear of flying and that fear extends to anything up high.

The Lions were based at the Sheraton Hotel and the team room was right at the top of the building – 30 stories up.

The players had to make at least five or six trips to their base at the top of the sky each day and Henderson's difficulty with heights was complicated by the fact that the elevators had glass walls.

Henderson, therefore, was not at all keen to make those trips and had to close his eyes on every occasion.

Neither was he willing to join his colleagues in a dip with the apparently harmless Tiger Sharks at a Brisbane Marine Park. "A shark is a shark in any man's language," he said.

The build up to the game was more intense than the opening matches and Henderson, selected at inside centre, admitted to have been more nervous than usual.

"I imagine it was just the hype that took place before the match. The Australian press appeared to be building us up for a fall. It was pointed out to us on more than one occasion that we had beaten nothing up to then. This was to be our first big test and people were saying we would run into problems."

As the following account indicates, these difficulties never arose although subsequent charges would be made against the 2001 team, all of which were refuted by tour manager Donal Lenihan

Match 3: Queensland.
Ballymore, Brisbane, June 16.
Attendance: 19,695. Weather: Dry, warm. Pitch: Firm.

QUEENSLAND 8 (S. Cordingly try, E. Flatley penalty) BRITISH AND IRISH LIONS 42 (B. O'Driscoll, R. Hill, D. James, R. Henderson, D. Luger try each, J. Wilkinson 3 penalties, 4 conversions)

QUEENSLAND captain Daniel Herbert saw enough from the British and Irish Lions to realise the all-conquering Wallabies were soon to face the biggest challenge of their lives.

Herbert was stunned at the efficiency of the Lions as they romped to another record-breaking victory at Ballymore.

The local supporters were equally as surprised at how efficiently the Lions broke the Queensland challenge in the opening half and left the Super 12 semi-finalists with an impossible second half task.

Queensland trailed 3-29 at the break but were credited at least with a stronger second half display.

Herbert, however, was not quite sure whether that was due to an improvement from his side or whether the Lions just sat back and relaxed in the knowledge that the game was well and truly won.

"I just don't know how much they were holding back. It is obvious they are a very good side but they might have just decided not to show their hand any more because of the upcoming Test games," he said at the time.

But Herbert was not totally distraught either as he left to join the Australian party to prepare for the opening international.

"I don't feel any different after this than I did before. Australia is a totally different team to Queensland. We know now that we are going to be in a dogfight but we have achieved a lot in the last few years and I feel we are still capable of achievement and of beating anybody.

"One thing is sure though, it will be a very interesting series and the Lions are better than anyone could have expected."

Though vastly more experienced in international terms than Ireland's Brian O'Driscoll, Herbert was full of praise for the Blackrock man who ghosted past him for the only Lions try of the second half. "God, that guy has a turn of pace. I didn't even see him coming and he was in for the try under the sticks. It will be an interesting Test confrontation."

O'Driscoll played alongside Henderson in the centre and the new Munster signing did his chances of playing in the first Test no harm at all with a superb all-round display.

His first half try may well have been a feature but it was his strength in the tackle and his ability to hold himself up and off-load that impressed coach Graham Henry most. "He certainly put his hands up and suggested he wanted a place. I like that in a player."

Another fighting for a Test place was Martin Corry, the man who came out as a replacement for the unfortunate Simon Taylor.

"I think he gave us selectors a little message that we may have made a mistake by not choosing him in the first place," said Henry.

This was the first chance of striking a blow for Test places in many respects, even though Henry said more than once that the team to meet New South Wales was to be closer to the mark.

O'Driscoll and Keith Wood - what a delightful little chip to allow Daffyd James score an important first half try for the Lions – had their names pencilled in even before this match. They merely proved the point that they could not be excluded.

Henderson moved ever closer, but at that particular stage of the tour the other Irish representatives, Malcolm O'Kelly, Jeremy Davidson and Ronan O'Gara, must have seen the writing on the wall.

Captain Martin Johnson was happy to have come through his first match unscathed, despite an early bout of punching against Queensland.

Johnson, publicly at least, suggested there was room for improvement despite racking up the highest Lions score ever against traditionally difficult Queensland.

"One of the things we have to learn quickly is the interpretation of the laws at the rucks. We had a bit of difficulty about that with a southern hemisphere referee. I'm not criticising Stuart Dickinson but we got a bit frustrated at times in the second half. We just need to talk to referees more before games and then do it their way. I'm sure there will be several meetings prior to the coming games."

But if Johnson was unhappy with the Lions' performance at ruck time in the second period, Herbert disagreed. "I thought that was one particular area they excelled in. If Martin is saying he was unhappy and there is room for improvement, that's a bit scary.

Queensland actually took the lead early on in this game but they struggled to win possession throughout the opening half. Once Wilkinson paved the way for a Dan Luger try in 17 minutes, it all went downhill for the home side.

Remarkably, the Lions kicked their first penalty goal of the tour six minutes later and that was probably proof that they held Queensland in much higher regard than either of their first two opposing teams. They set out to play controlled rugby rather than exhibition stuff but managed, at times, to combine the two.

A 30th minute Rob Henderson try and a 33rd minute penalty from Wilkinson pushed the lead out to 18-3, and in injury time the tourists scored twice to flatten the Reds.

O'Driscoll's superb second half try was the signal for the Lions to ease up. The game was won at that stage and they never really struggled although they were fighting a rearguard action for much of the second half.

Lions defence coach Phil Larder would have been proud of the way they defended until Queensland scored their only try 12 minutes from time.

The Reds had high hopes of enhancing their proud record. In 1971, when the Lions stopped off en-route to New Zealand, Queensland beat them 15-11 and they pushed the 1989 team all the way before losing narrowly.

After 40 minutes of this game there was never going to be a scary repeat.

SCORING SEQUENCE
FIRST HALF

12 mins - Elton Flatley penalty. 3-0 to Queensland.

17 mins - Dan Luger try. 5-3 to Lions.

23 mins - Johnny Wilkinson penalty. 8-3.

30 mins - Rob Henderson try, Wilkinson conversion. 15-3.

33 mins - Wilkinson penalty. 18-3.

41 mins - Daffyd James try, Wilkinson conversion. 25-3.

46 mins - Richard Hill try, Wilkinson conversion. 32-3.

SECOND HALF

3 mins - Brian O'Driscoll try, Wilkinson conversion. 39-3.

13 mins - Wilkinson penalty. 42-3.

28 mins - Sam Cordingly try. 42-8.

QUEENSLAND: M. Tabrett, J. Pelesasa, D. Herbert (captain), S. Kefu, D. McCallum, E. Flatley, S. Cordingly, N. Stiles, M. Foley, G. Panaho, N. Sharpe, M. Connors, M. Cockbain, T. Kefu, D. Croft. Replacements. J. Ramsamy for S. Kefu (53), S. Hardman for Foley (62), S. Kerr for Stiles (65), M. Mitchell for Sharpe (injured, 71), J. Roe for Cockbain (75).

BRITISH AND IRISH LIONS: I. Balshaw (England), D. James (Wales), B. O'Driscoll (Ireland), R. Henderson (Ireland), D. Luger (England), J. Wilkinson (England), R. Howley (Wales), T. Smith (Scotland), K. Wood (Ireland), P. Vickery (England), M. Johnson (England (captain), D. Grewcock (England), R. Hill (England), M. Corry (England), N. Back (England). Replacements. M. Dawson (England) for Howley (injured, 47), J. Robinson (England) for O'Driscoll (injured, 61), C. Charvis (Wales) for Back (71), S. Murray (Scotland) for Johnson (77).

Referee. S. Dickinson (Australia).

Lions record against Queensland

1899: The Lions 3 Queensland 11
1904: The Lions 24 Queensland 5
1930: the Lions 26 Queensland 16
1959: The Lions 39 Queensland 11
1966: The Lions 26 Queensland 3
1971: The Lions 11 Queensland 15
1989: The Lions 19 Queensland 15
2001: The Lions 42 Queensland 8

Ronan O'Gara on the attack

O'Gara cranking up for another successful goal-kick

Rob Henderson scores a spectacular try

215

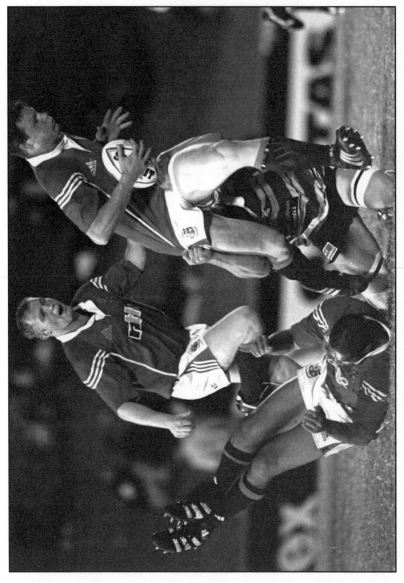

Malcolm O'Kelly gallops through a tackle on the way to scoring a try

Happiness is .... Holding a Koala Bear and relaxing on the beach. Brian O'Driscoll relaxes in a wildlife sanctuary and on the beach at Manly with buddy Keith Wood

CHAPTER 17

RING THE WARNING BELL

LIONS tour manager Donal Lenihan stood shoulder to shoulder with his players and showed determination that Australian rabble-rousers wouldn't disrupt any plans made to take on the Wallabies in the three match Test Series.

Lenihan vowed not to let Australia A coach Eddie Jones or anyone else get in the way of the goals set by the Lions, although Jones pulled off a coup when he helped inspire his side to a shock victory at the NorthPower Stadium in Gosford.

In the build up to the game, the former Irish international and now Lions team manager was upset at suggestions from Jones that the Lions would try to bully their way through the Test series

Lenihan remarked: "I don't quite know what Eddie Jones was trying to achieve. It may be a case of trying to fire his team up but we have watched the video of the game against Queensland a number of times. Sure, there were some incidents in the early stages of the game but we did not set out to create any trouble.

"You have to draw your own conclusions because we were not the ones to start the problems, such as they were.

"I keep emphasising the fact that we were not the aggressors in any way during that match so I really don't know what their coach is talking about.

"You can talk to any player in this party and at no stage has there been mention of a physical battle, taking out the Australians or causing difficulties at the start of any game."

"It seems very strange that this thing is stretching on and more comments have been made since the initial ones.

"Our approach to this match is going to be the same as we had for the first three games, but the comments that have been made will make us even more determined to get it right on the night.

"Sometimes, you hear comments like this second hand but there can be no getting away from the fact that this should be taken out of context. I mean, you can't take things out of context when someone issues a press release on the issue!

"Really though, there has been enough talk about this and I think the whole Lions party just want to get on with the game."

There was, in any event, no retribution off the field on foot of all the allegations from Jones.

Lenihan explained: "There is a commissioner there to judge whether a player from one side or the other, or players from both sides, should be called before a tribunal. Nobody was. We are not going to pursue the matter and nobody else has either so I really don't know what the fuss is all about."

Lenihan was not happy with the fact that the Australian Rugby Union had their way to have home based referees take charge of six out of the ten games. "I was concerned with the fact that an agreement had been put in place and was not honoured. The International Board made a ruling eventually and we will have to stick by that."

In the build-up to this game, though probably not after it, Lenihan believed the battle for Test places had intensified and even mentioned two replacement players in his summation.

"It has been an eye-opener to see the likes of Martin Corry and Gordon Bulloch, not original selections, come out here and throw down the gauntlet. You have to respect that kind of determination.

"Before we arrived here, we went through a team-building process in England and it was done in an attempt to create a one team outlook even though there are so many more players that can take the field.

"It would be naïve to think that the guy who doesn't make the Test team won't be hugely disappointed, but I do believe that in the professional era, all the players have bought into the concept of winning the Test series and are prepared to do anything to help us achieve that."

The single most difficult preparatory game for that Test series began in Gosford.

Australia picked a very strong team to face the Lions and were together for a full week in preparation, an unusually long period for an A side to prepare. In the end, it paid off as the following account of the match reveals.

Match 4: Australia A.
NorthPower Stadium, Gosford, June 19.
Attendance: 23,043. Weather: Cool, dry. Pitch: Firm

AUSTRALIA A 28 (S. Stainforth try, M. Edmonds 7 penalties, conversion) BRITISH AND IRISH LIONS 25 (M. Taylor, M. Perry, J. Robinson try each, N. Jenkins 2 penalties, M. Dawson 2 conversions)

SO the 2001 British and Irish Lions are not as good as they thought they were! The sequence of record-breaking victories they established in the opening games of the tour was brought to a shuddering half in Gosford.

The emerging Wallabies struck a major blow for Australian rugby in advance of the Test series.

The final score suggests a hotly disputed contest. It was anything but, and it took two injury time tries to put a respectable look on things.

Nothing will disguise the fact that the Lions were shockingly inept for most of the contest.

Coach Graham Henry had hoped a number of players would put their names forward for Test selection. Most simply wrote themselves out of the equation.

From start virtually to finish, the Lions found themselves on the back foot against a physical Australia A side that played with purpose, passion and skill.

The Lions trailed by just nine points at the interval. Given their inability to secure or keep possession, that was a near miracle.

Australia disrupted their scrum, destroyed them out of touch and won virtually all of the re-starts.

Mistakes abounded as they tried desperately to pick up the pieces and the Wallabies played all of the football.

The Lions defence was continuously stretched, but to their credit it held firm for 60 minutes until Australia scored a marvellous opening try from centre Scott Staniforth.

That was the one area that Henry was happy with. He certainly wasn't pleased about the succession of errors his side made and the staggering penalty count against them.

The Lions conceded 24 penalties and then had Lawrence Dallaglio sent to the sin-bin for constantly joining the rucks from the wrong side.

"We have a lot of work to do in the line outs and even more to get to grips with what is and is not allowed at ruck time," conceded Henry.

Team manager Donal Lenihan insisted there was no criticism of referee Paul Honiss but agreed that the squad would have to quickly come to grips with the interpretations of southern hemisphere referees.

There really wasn't a single member of the pack to stand out although Scott Quinnell, Martyn Williams and Dallaglio did their best. Against that, Tom Bowman, Phil Waugh and Jim Williams (a major coup for Munster) were monumental.

In frustration, Henry substituted hooker Robin McBryde with Gordon Bulloch early in the second half, but the supply of ball from lineouts was still minimal and the Lions ultimately lost nine of their own throws.

With scant possession, the Lions back division never really functioned in the way they had in the three previous matches. Jason Robinson looked easily the best of a pretty poor lot and Neil Jenkins and Ben Cohen were the worst of them.

The game was up for Mike Catt who had a recurrence of his calf muscle strain and the injury forced him to miss the rest of a tour he hardly participated in.

Henry might have done better with his substitutions. The decision to move Austin Healey to out half and introduce Matt Dawson produced no improvement. With Ronan O'Gara on the bench; Dawson took over the goal-kicking duties and missed two crucial kicks that could have turned the tide. O'Gara surely would have done the business better and might have saved this match.

Henry immediately set himself the task of improvement in just about every area, even with higher profile personnel.

This was the day the Lions entered the real world of Australian rugby.

"Perhaps we were living a bit in fantasy land after the first three games. This was reality and we had better get used to it," admitted the coach.

Many more felt exactly the same.

SCORING SEQUENCE
FIRST HALF

9 mins - Neil Jenkins penalty. 3-0 to Lions.

13 mins - Manuel Edmonds penalty. 3-3.

23 mins - Edmonds penalty. 6-3.

29 mins - Jenkins penalty. 6-6.

34 mins - Edmonds penalty. 9-6.

36 mins - Edmonds penalty. 12-6.

40 mins - Edmonds penalty. 15-6.

SECOND HALF

18 mins - Scott Staniforth try, Edmonds conversion. 22-6.

21 mins - Mark Taylor try, Matt Dawson conversion. 22-13.

23 mins - Edmonds penalty. 25-13.

35 mins - Edmonds penalty. 28-13.

40 mins - Matt Perry try. 28-18.

45 mins - Jason Robinson try, Dawson conversion. 28-25.

AUSTRALIA A: R. Graham (Queensland), M. Bartholomeusz (ACT), S. Staniforth (New South Wales), N. Gray (New South Wales), G. Bond (ACT), M. Edmonds (New South Wales), C. Whitaker (New South Wales), C. Blades (New South Wales), B. Cannon (New South Wales), R. Moore (New South Wales), T. Bowman (New South Wales), J. Harrison (ACT), D. Lyons (New South Wales), J. Williams (ACT), P. Waugh (New South Wales). Replacements. James Holbeck (ACT) for Graham (25, injured), S. Payne (New South Wales) for Whitaker (55), P. Noriego (New South Wales) for Blades (62), J. West (New South Wales) for Bowman (66), P. Ryan (ACT) for Williams (71), T. Murphy (ACT) for Cannon (74).

BRITISH AND IRISH LIONS: M. Perry (England), B. Cohen (England), W. Greenwood (England), M. Catt (England), J. Robinson (England), N. Jenkins (Wales), A. Healey (England), J. Leonard (England), R. McBryde (Wales), D. Young (Wales) Captain; S. Murray (Scotland), M. O'Kelly (Ireland), L. Dallaglio (England), S. Quinnell (Wales), M. Williams (Wales). Replacements. M. Taylor (Wales) for Catt (45, injured), G. Bullock (Scotland) for McBryde, J. Davidson (Ireland) for O'Kelly (both 52), M. Dawson (England) for Jenkins (56), D. Morris (Wales) for Young (69).Temporary. C. Charvis (Wales) for Quinnell (34-41).

Referee. P. Honiss (New Zealand).

Lions Record v Australia A

1989: The Lions 23 Australia A 18
2001: The Lions 25 Australia A 28

CHAPTER 18

BATTERED, BRUISED
BUT VICTORIOUS

THE Sydney suburb of Manly was the base for the Lions in the build up to the game with New South Wales.

It proved the perfect choice for those who wanted to relax. The Lions stayed in the Manly Pacific Parkroyal, a beachfront property flanked by chic cafes and bars and all the beautiful people.

Whilst not training, they were afforded the opportunity of a quiet stroll along the beach, a bit of surfing or just general rest and relaxation although relaxation was never on Graham Henry's agenda.

For those who wanted a livelier night-life (players excluded), the Manly to Sydney Ferry point was just a short walk and a 30 minute ferry ride away.

It helped that the weather was glorious and on June 21, for instance, the shortest day of the year in Australia, temperatures of 21 degrees Celsius were recorded. This was THE life in June of 2001.

The pressure was mounting on the Lions, however. Mike Catt and Lawrence Dallaglio were diagnosed with injuries so serious that they would have to return home.

225

The Australian press continued harping on about illegalities perpetrated by the Lions before Donal Lenihan and Graham Henry finally responded with vigorous denials.

Assistant coach Andy Robinson set the ball rolling when he attacked Australian referees for not allowing the Lions scrummage.

"Scrummaging is an important part of the game. The way they look at it, it appears to be more like Rugby League. We are not allowed to contest the scrums because we get penalised at every second one. They will have to look seriously at this because the laws state that you are, in fact, allowed to scrummage. We will be talking to the referees about this because we have to get it sorted out."

Match 5: New South Wales.
Sydney Football Ground, June 23.
Attendance: 41,068. Weather: Warm. Pitch: Firm.

NEW SOUTH WALES 24 (M. Edmonds try, 2 conversions, S. Pinkerton, F. Cullimore, S. Harris try each) BRITISH AND IRISH LIONS 41 (J. Wilkinson try, 4 conversions, 2 penalties, J. Robinson 2 tries, B. O'Driscoll, D. James try each, M. Dawson conversion)

IT was a match marred by violence, sparked off by New South Wales. It was a game of controversy and one not greeted well by outspoken coach Bob Dwyer.

Duncan McRae smashed Ireland out half Ronan O'Gara and that particular incident made a mockery of all the illegal taunts about the Lions.

At the Sydney Football Ground in front of a huge 41,000 crowd, McRae struck O'Gara eleven times, nine of them at least when his opponent was defenceless. It was a "great" inducement to get parents get their kids involved in the game.

226

The upshot of it all was that McRae was suspended for seven weeks, three more than he might have expected but five less than he deserved.

Questioned in the aftermath of this match, Dwyer admitted that McRae had gone way too far even in the face of suggested provocation – hotly denied by O'Gara, the Lions management and, on the basis of judgement, the citing commissioner as well.

"Duncan has apologised for throwing quite a few punches - which would be very difficult to deny - but he said he retaliated. I have had a brief look at it on the replays and he says he retaliated at what he thought was a swinging arm in the ruck situation.

"Unfortunately, you can only see the player's arm swinging and don't see any contact being made. Duncan took offence at it and lashed out."

Dwyer, famous for his 1992 remarks about Irish and Munster prop Peter Clohessy, tried his best to play down the incident and pointed out that Danny Grewcock and Phil Vickery had traded the first blows of the game, albeit a good 40 minutes before.

The facts state that Tom Bowman was issued with a yellow card inside the first 30 seconds.

"McRae has admitted he was wrong and he will be punished for that but the Lions threw a few cheap shots out there as well," said Dwyer.

Those comments cut no ice with Lions manager Donal Lenihan who branded New South Wales, and particularly McRae, a disgrace.

"It was quite clear that the guy came in and whacked Ronan O'Gara. I'm quite sure, if we did that, we would know what type of headlines to expect in Australia. If one of our players got involved in an incident like that, we would be reading it for the next twelve years.

"He was opened up in two places - badly - and so much so that he could not come back on the field. It wasn't just a reactionary punch, it was a flurry of punches which would have done justice to any top class boxer."

McRae was sent off and five other players, three from New South Wales and two from the Lions, were shown yellow cards during the course of a fractious match obviously set up to soften up the tourists in advance of the first Test in Brisbane a week on.

While Dwyer denied this was the case, New South Wales captain Phil Waugh suggested it might have been.

Still, he believed there was an over-reaction when four players were sent to the sin-bin after the one incident involving the group.

"We wanted to test them in advance of their match against Australia. It was a pretty physical contest and I honestly felt that there was no need to send four players to the sin-bin in the second half."

Most people would probably agree with that on the basis that it was a handbag type of punch-up and the lack of players ruined the structure of the game for the subsequent ten, and maybe more, minutes.

O'Gara was later paraded for the cameras, sporting a badly swollen eye which required eight stitches to two different wounds. McRae obviously did a good job.

What irked O'Gara more than anything was that McRae, formerly of Saracens, didn't even apologise, either after the game or following his appearance before the citing commissioner whom O'Gara also met on the Sunday morning.

While McRae expressed regret to the commissioner, he never said a word to O'Gara and he had every opportunity to do so.

In any event, it did not affect the Lions as they proceeded to record another victory on the ten-match tour.

After being beaten by Australia A, victory over New South Wales was imperative to get the tour back on track.

They achieved that with a measure of excellence even if the match was thrown into chaos when the teams were reduced to 13 and 12 respectively for a ten minute period in the second half.

Referee Scott Young asked touch-judge Stuart Dickinson if he was serious when the suggestion was made he send four players-two from either side - to the sin-bin.

The four walked and the game lost all shape.

But the Lions, apart from a wobbly period early in the second half, were still always well in control.

Will Greenwood's injury ruled him out of contention for a place in the team for the first Test – further good news for Rob Henderson - but Jonny Wilkinson always got the best out of a back division where Brian O'Driscoll starred.

O'Driscoll scored another smashing try, and if Dwyer was defensive in his stance on the McRae issue he took the opportunity to warn Wallaby coach Rod Macqueen – as if he needed warning – about O'Driscoll.

"He is something really special, isn't he? He has tremendous ability, pace and vision and will be one of the key men in this Lions Test side."

Dwyer could never have spoken truer words.

SCORING SEQUENCE
FIRST HALF

4 mins - Brian O'Driscoll try, Jonny Wilkinson conversion. 7-0.

7 mins - Stuart Pinkerton try. 7-5.

16 mins - Jason Robinson try. Wilkinson conversion. 14-5.

32 mins - Wilkinson penalty. 17-5.

37 mins - Robinson try, Wilkinson conversion. 24-5.

SECOND HALF

6 mins - Francis Cullimore try. 24-10.

12 mins - Sam Harris try, Manuel Edmonds conversion. 24-17.

20 mins - Wilkinson penalty. 27-17.

26 mins - Wilkinson try and conversion. 34-17.

34 mins - Daffyd James try, Matt Dawson conversion. 41-17.

44 mins - Edmonds try, conversion. 41-24.

NEW SOUTH WALES . D. McRae, F. Cullimore, L. Inman, S. Harris, S. Qau Qau, M. Edmonds, S. Payne, C. Blades, B. Cannon, R. Moore, J. West, T. Bowman, S. Pinkerton, F. Finau, P. Waugh (captain). Replacements. P. Besseling for Bowman (half time), P. Noriego for Blades (43), R. Tombs for Edmonds (66), E. Carter for Pinkerton (70).

BRITISH AND IRISH LIONS: I. Balshaw (England), D. James (Wales), B. O'Driscoll (Ireland), W. Greenwood (England), J. Robinson (England), J. Wilkinson (England), M. Dawson (England), D. Morris (Wales), K. Wood (Ireland), P. Vickery (England), M. Johnson (England, captain), D. Grewcock (England), L. Dallaglio (England), S. Quinnell (Wales), N. Back (England). Replacements. R. O'Gara (Ireland) for Greenwood (24, injured), T.

Smith (Scotland) for Quinnell (58), M. Perry (England) for O'Gara (61 injured), R. Hill (England) for Back (72), A. Healey (England) for Wilkinson (74), R. McBryde (Wales) for Wood (78)

Referee. S. Young (Queensland).

Lions record against New South Wales
1899:	The Lions 4 New South Wales 3	
	The Lions 11 New South Wales 5	
1904:	The Lions 27 New South Wales 0	
	The Lions 29 New South Wales 6	
	The Lions 5 New South Wales 0	
1930:	The Lions 29 New South Wales 10	
	The Lions 3 New South Wales 28	
1950:	The Lions 22 New South Wales 6	
	The Lions 12 New South Wales 17	
1959:	The Lions 14 New South Wales 18	
1966:	The Lions 6 New South Wales 6	
1971:	The Lions 14 New South Wales 12	
1989:	The Lions 23 New South Wales 21	
2001:	The Lions 41 New South Wales 24	

CHAPTER 19

VICTORY AND THE DEATH
OF A LEGEND

THIS should have been a happy time of the tour. The backdrop was wonderful, the weather magnificent and the atmosphere relaxed in a town graced with marvellous resort hotels and beautiful beaches.

Instead, the mood in the camp was sombre following the tragic and sudden death of one of two Australian Rugby Union Liaison Officers, Anton Toia, the day before the game.

Anton was a diplomat, a bagman, a rub man, political and rugby advisor to anyone who cared to listen. Most people did.

He had been involved with virtually every international team to tour Australia over a period of more than ten years. He was, in essence, a permanent fixture and built up a rapport with international players from most rugby nations during that time.

He was particularly fond of the Irish because, although a New Zealand Maori who had settled in Australia for over 30 years, he was immensely proud of the fact that he had and Irish grandmother from County Fermanagh.

When Ireland toured Australia in 1994 and 1999, Anton busied himself and often worked long into the night to ensure the

232

teams were given every facility to help them try to beat the Wallabies at a particularly difficult time in Irish rugby.

It is a measure of the esteem in which the international rugby community held him that Scotland invited him to become their official baggage master for the 1999 World Cup held in Europe.

He was a man with an ever-present, impish smile. He liked a drink, a smoke and a bit of craic as well as the odd catnap at unusual times of the day.

On Monday June 26, Anton and fellow Liaison Officer Dick Hart prevailed on a friend to bring them and some of the players out whale watching. It was a bright, sunny day. Two hundred yards from shore Anton, who was a former champion swimmer, dived off the boat and decided to swim in to put some beers on ice.

Waist deep in water, he waved to his friends to inform them he had made it safely back. When the boat docked there was no sign of Anton. Minutes later, his body was found face down in the sea by two surfers. He died of a massive heart attack.

Many tears were shed; by those who knew him well and those who had met him for the first time on this 2001 tour.

Rugby lost a great man and all those who knew him lost a great friend. May he Rest In Peace.

Match 6: New South Wales Country
Coffs Harbour International Sports Stadium, June 26.
Attendance: 9,972. Weather: Warm, dry. Pitch: Firm.

NEW SOUTH WALES COUNTRY 3 (N. Croft penalty) BRITISH AND IRISH LIONS 46 (B. Cohen 2 tries, C. Charvis, S. Gibbs, A. Healey, D. Young try each, N. Jenkins 5 conversions, 2 penalties)

THE Lions were inevitable winners but this display at the Coffs Harbour International Sports Stadium will not rank as their most memorable hour.

Coach Graham Henry put his finger on the pulse when he said: "it was a bit of a shambles of a match, fragmented and hardly well directed. It was a poor game of rugby and a frustrating one to play in. There were patches when we looked fair enough but we didn't play that well."

Henry excused his players on one basis, however, and that was the performance of referee Greg Hinton.

"Have they changed the rules?" he asked.

"The rucks and mauls were an absolute shambles. There were bodies everywhere in offside positions and that certainly stopped the continuity of the match. The opposition certainly appear to have set out to keep the score down and they did that pretty effectively.

"Full credit to them, they got away with it but it was pretty disappointing from our point of view. There were too many stoppages and too many penalties to allow the game to flow."

But Henry insisted that credit should also be given to the home team. "I thought they played very well at times. They put it up to us and they were pretty determined that they didn't want to be swept aside. There were times we created good passages of play but they defended against them very well. It should not be forgotten that there were two sides out there, and they were a team that didn't look like rolling over. For that, they deserve a pat on the back."

Manager Donal Lenihan looked forward to the Test series and to the intervention of top class referees.

"I'm getting fed up talking about referees because it has been going on for a number of weeks. As Graham has said, there was no continuity in this game because of difficulties in and around the rucks and mauls. We want to get on with playing football in games where experienced referees are involved."

Lenihan believes part of the problems faced by the Lions in failing to completely put away a competitive but inexperienced Country side may have stemmed from the tragic death of Anton Toia.

"Normally you lay down plans for a game on the eve of a game but nobody felt like talking about rugby after that so everything was cancelled. It must have affected the players in some way because Anton was a super guy and was liked and admired by everyone in the squad.

"At the end of the day, I suppose there are no real excuses for failing to achieve what we set out to achieve - and that was a bigger win than the one we got. We never had any trouble in winning but we could have done it more clinically."

Captain Dai Young admitted to have been frustrated throughout the game. "We had to ask the referee on several occasions for the reasons why we were being penalised and sometimes why they weren't. They were slowing the ball down, holding on in the tackle and we weren't able to keep the ball for five or six phases. We therefore were not able to mount enough attacks and to get a game plan going."

One of the major success stories of the game, though, was Welsh centre Scott Gibbs in his first game of the tour.

A surprise exclusion in the first instance, Gibbs has joined the tour as replacement for the injured Mike Catt.

"He hit the tour running and seems to want to prove a point to us," admitted Henry.

Others to rise above the general low standard exhibited in the game were Tyrone Howe, Ben Cohen, Mark Taylor, Martin Corry, Colin Charvis, Jeremy Davidson and, occasionally, Malcolm O'Kelly.

But it became increasingly clear that none of this side would in the starting team for the opening Test. Front-runner Iain Balshaw had a lot to prove but he really proved nothing other than a loss of form.

In relation to the match, the Lions struggled to score for long periods. Neil Jenkins did kick them into the lead early on but they had to wait 25 minutes for an opening try before cutting loose in the closing ten minutes of the first half.

Having established a 29-3 half-time lead, the fans waited for the floodgates to open. They never did and could only tack on 17 points in the second half. Poor fare indeed as New South Wales Country offered dogged resistance and the Lions played well beneath their potential.

On a happier note, the Wallace family from Ireland wrote themselves into the history books when they became the first family to provide three brothers to the British and Irish Lions.

David Wallace arrived as a replacement for the injured Lawrence Dallaglio prior to this match and hours later pulled on a Lions jersey for the first time

Wallace came on as a second half replacement for Martin Corry even though he had just concluded a near 40-hour journey from Copenhagen to London through Singapore and Sydney before arriving in Coffs Harbour.

He was on his way to Poland via Copenhagen for an Irish two-week summer training camp and heard the news through Ronan O'Gara when he turned on his mobile telephone for a few minutes at the airport.

"Rog said to me would be see me in the next couple of days and I thought immediately that he was leaving the Lions tour, not me joining. It was a big shock but a great surprise. Don't say this too loud, but it's a bad break to have had to miss Poland. All my friends are out there!"

"My luggage was sent straight through to Poland. It's now out there somewhere but it doesn't worry me where it is," he said after the game.

"What counts is that I am in Australia and it is a great honour. It's fantastic to have been able to follow in the footsteps of Richard and Paul and even better if it is a family record."

The circumstances of English hooker Dorian West's arrival – on the same day - as a replacement hooker were even more bizarre because he had just arrived in Menorca to start a family holiday.

"I just got into the airport and got a telephone call from Martin Johnson to tell me. I picked up my bags, dropped the wife and kids off at our villa and went straight back to the airport. I have a funny feeling she is not too pleased with me at the moment.

"I had to head for Frankfurt and then on to Singapore before arriving here."

"I thought at one stage I was being called on and was warming up before the end of the game - using a matchstick to keep my eyelids apart. It would have been nice because I don't know at this stage whether I will get a chance. With a bit of luck, I will.

"I had better, because if the wife finds out I just came here for a bit of a holiday, I might as well not go home at all. In any event, I'll have to take her on a second holiday so this trip might cost me more money than I make!"

SCORING SEQUENCE
FIRST HALF

7 mins - Neil Jenkins penalty. 3-0.

23 mins - Nathan Croft penalty. 3-3

25 mins - Ben Cohen try. 8-3.

32 mins - Colin Charvis try, Jenkins conversion. 15-3.

36 mins - Scott Gibbs try, Jenkins conversion. 22-3.

41 mins - Austin Healey try, Jenkins conversion. 29-3.

SECOND HALF

1 min - Neil Jenkins penalty. 32-3.

5 mins - Dai Young try, Jenkins conversion. 39-3.

22 mins - Ben Cohen try, Jenkins conversion. 46-3.

NEW SOUTH WALES COUNTRY: N. Croft, V. Tailasa, R. MacDougal, K. Shepherd, W. Crosby, C. Doyle, R. Petty, A. Baldwin, J. McCormack, M. Bowman, D. Lubans, B. Wright, B. Dale, B. Klasen (captain), C. Taylor. Replacements. G. Refshauge for Wright (58), D. Dimmock for Taylor (59), D. Banovich for Crosby (61), M. Browne for Shepherd, J. Vaalotu for McCormack (both 66), D. Thomas for Baldwin (70).

BRITISH AND IRISH LIONS: I. Balshaw (England), B. Cohen (England), M. Taylor (Wales), S. Gibbs (Wales), T. Howe (Ireland), N. Jenkins (Wales), A. Healey (England), J. Leonard (England), G. Bulloch (Scotland), D. Young (Wales) captain; J. Davidson (Ireland), M. O'Kelly (Ireland), C. Charvis (Wales), M. Corry (England), M. Williams (Wales). Replacements. D. Wallace (Ireland) for Corry (56), D. Morris (Wales) for Leonard (57), S. Murray (Scotland) for O'Kelly (70), Temporary replacement, R. O'Gara (Ireland) for Gibbs (46-57).

Referee. G. Hinton (Queensland).

Lions record against New South Wales Country

1959: The Lions 27 New South Wales Country 14
1966: The Lions 6 New South Wales Country 3
1989: The Lions 72 New South Wales Country 13
2001: The Lions 46 New South Wales Country 3

Other matches against New South Wales Country teams.
1899:   The Lions 11 New South Wales Central/Southern 3
           The Lions 19 New South Wales Western Districts 0
1904:   The Lions 21 New South Wales Western Unions 6
           The Lions 17 New South Wales Northern Unions 3

CHAPTER 20

GABBA GLORY

IT is not often the Australian Rugby Union gets things wrong but they certainly seemed to have miscalculated by choosing to play the opening game of the Test series in Brisbane.

Australia, out of 17 previous Test games against the Lion, had only won three times. All of those victories were in Sydney.

In terms of capacity, the Gabba, an Australian Rules ground being used as a rugby venue for the very first time, was the smallest ground of the three Test venues that allowed the huge Lions supporters group turn the fixture into what was effectively a home match.

The heat was off the Lions in the build up to the game. Prior to departure for Australia and for some time after their arrival, they had had been installed as favourites to win the series.

The defeat by Australia A in the fourth game put things in a different perspective. Former Wallaby players, supporters and the bookmakers all agreed that the World Champions had the ability to win.

David Campese, the man who has never been allowed forget a blunder that gifted the Lions a third Test and series victory in 1989, tipped Australia to win by at least ten points.

He expected the Lions to provide problems up front but believed the Australian backs would be too clever and too powerful for the visitors.

Campese viewed the injuries to Dan Luger and Lawrence Dallaglio, and their subsequent unavailability, as huge blows from which the Lions would not recover.

"The backline has been weakened by Luger's absence and it hasn't helped that Iain Balshaw has lost his form. The back row is a hugely important area and I expect the Lions will miss the influence of Dallaglio."

Campese tipped centres Daniel Herbert and Nathan Gray to blitz Rob Henderson and Brian O'Driscoll.

"O'Driscoll, especially, and Henderson are very good players but they are up against two really great players. They will find it hard."

Overall, Campese said the Wallaby back division had a more rounded look about it. "I just think they will prove too strong for the Lions."

In the days leading up to this first match, sections of the Australian media attempted to drag up dirt on the Lions by harping back to 1989 when the touring side were accused of foul tactics in their successful bid to win the series.

Finlay Calder, the 1989 captain, was in Australia following the 2001 Lions categorically denied, not for the first time, that his side had set out to intimidate the Wallabies twelve years before.

He admitted there were unsavoury incidents in that Test series but felt saddened that the series is remembered for anything other than the good rugby played by both sides on that tour.

"Look, I'm not proclaiming innocence on behalf of my team but there were two sides to the story.

"Having said that, the game has moved on since then. There was a share of dirty play in rugby a decade or so ago. All that has changed. The game has moved on. It's a professional sport now and video cameras are in place to catch people involved in dirty play. Players are more conscious nowadays of their responsibilities and I am certain that this series will be played in a sporting manner without the aggression of the past."

The publicity clearly irked Lions manager Donal Lenihan who asked that the book on the controversial 1989 series be closed.

His plea went on deaf ears. On the morning of the game, a headline in the Courier Mail newspaper in Brisbane screamed "REFEREE PREPARED FOR FIRST-MINUTE SEND-OFF."

South African Andre Watson was quoted as saying; "Dirty play will not be tolerated even in the so-called sorting out stages of the game. God forbid it happened. I would be happy to do what I have to do. If something ugly erupts, I'm going to deal with it. A lot of people may not like it but it's going to be the right thing to do, even in the first five minutes."

Watson, however, expressed the view that there would be no rows. "Look, these are big, professional players in a contact sport and they sometimes lose it in a reactionary sense. We're all human and I believe I will be able to handle things."

In contrast to Wallaby number eight Toutai Kefu (an old friend of Ireland's Trevor Brennan) who suggested there would indeed be a flare-up in the opening quarter, Lions skipper Martin Johnson expressed a desire to merely get on with the game.

"There have been a few isolated incidents on the tour. Quite frankly, I'm bored with all the chat. It's just a game of rugby and it will be hard enough without thinking about foul play."

Watson, meanwhile, took all the hype with a grain of salt. "People from both sides of the fence are making different statements, pointing to the threat of violence and highlighting illegalities on either side. It's a typical pre-game atmosphere in a build-up to a major game. I really don't take any notice of what is said before these type of matches. If I did, I don't think I should be refereeing. When the game starts, the slate is clean as far as I am concerned."

So it was. Watson allowed the game to flow, the players behaved themselves and the Lions supporters were treated to a magnificent spectacle.

A report in the Sydney Morning Herald turned the heat back on the Wallabies. The main headline read: LIONS SHAME COMPLACENT AUSTRALIANS. The match report, by Rugby Correspondent Greg Growden, argued that it wasn't a game but it was a shame.

"Many hours on, and Australian rugby fans are still wondering exactly what happened, how a side so proud of it's world champion status was made to look so brain dead by an opposition riddled with problems.

"It was obvious, however, even before kick-off that things were crook in the Wallaby nook. The janty Australians jogged out, bounding about as if they thought they only had to turn up to enjoy victory.

"For the next hour, it was a case it was a case of the Lions taking advantage of complacency, but with the added dagger of knowing exactly what Australia would do, while the Wallabies had no idea what the tourists were up to."

Campese bemoaned the lack of awareness in the Australian camp and he too suggested the Wallabies had taken the challenge too lightly.

"You can tell by a team's mood from the way they carry themselves. They ran onto the pitch with that air of 'this shouldn't be too tough'.

"There was talk about rough tactics but they never surfaced. It was a game readymade for TALES OF THE UNEXPECTED.

"The most pleasing aspect of the Lions win was that they didn't rely on muscle to get them through the Australian defence. They used the pace of Jason Robinson and centre Brian O'Driscoll.

"My view that the Lions would be too conservative was blown away in the first few minutes when Robinson left Chris Latham grabbing thin air.

"As for O'Driscoll, it was so refreshing to see a player at this level back himself with skill and speed. How many times do you see big blokes in midfield just running straight into each other? Not the Irishman. He ran to gaps and then went through them.

"The defence just didn't know how to shut him down and the try he scored was an absolute gem. You hardly ever see players in an international getting the ball and setting off to run half the field. This guy was pure class."

Match 7: Australia (First Test)
Gabba, Brisbane, June 30.
Attendance: 37,460. Weather: Warm, dry. Pitch: Greasy.

AUSTRALIA 13 (A. Walker try, penalty, N. Gray try) BRITISH AND IRISH LIONS 29 (J. Robinson, D. James, B. O'Driscoll, S. Quinnell try each, J. Wilkinson 3 conversions, penalty)

IF it were Hollywood, Ireland would not have three Oscar recipients after blitzing World champions Australia at the Gabba in Brisbane.

The three latest Irish Lions did their country proud. There were two Man of the Match Awards, one from the media and another through a telephone link with Sky television.

Keith Wood was the public's hero while Brian O'Driscoll came a close second from the press corps. There were lots of mentions for Rob Henderson, a brilliant contributor to a brilliant night in the history of the British and Irish Lions.

Not one of the three, or the others besides, gloated at an unexpectedly high victory over the World champions. But hell, they could have done.

Praise was heaped upon the Irish contingent and most of it came from unexpected quarters - England.

Former Lions Jeremy Guscott and Gareth Chilcott reacted favourably. As a front rower, Chilcott delighted in the performance of Wood. "He was everywhere that guy. What a performance!"

Guscott, a match-winner in South Africa four years before, believes O'Driscoll to be the new voice of Irish and world rugby. "He was absolutely out of this world. One of the great attributes that marked him out from others is that he has pace off a static start. It is very difficult to stop him because he takes off like grease lightening.

"His second half try was an absolute classic. I didn't think it was possible for someone to crash through and then weave away from the Wallaby defence like that. I mean, they pride themselves - and justifiably so - as having the best defence in the world."

Henderson was equally lauded. A smiling former triumphant Lions captain, Finlay Calder remarked: "That boy Henderson was a revelation. He was one of the players in the Lions team I worried about. I realise that he has been in top form but I did not expect him to be able to make the step up. He took the Australians on in a big way and defended brilliantly.

"He has put down the marker for the tour as one player determined to nail down a place in the side and keep it. That is the beauty of Lions tours. You always get someone who comes from nowhere. He hasn't exactly come from nowhere but I would not have fancied his chances of making the Test side before this. Now, well he is there to stay, isn't he?"

In a most dispassionate way, looking back on the contribution of these three guys makes you feel proud to be Irish.

The audacious Wood stormed through the game and even had an attempt at a drop goal in the second half. It was on target but unfortunately not long enough.

O'Driscoll scored a try and helped make another with a brilliant run, while Henderson bashed his way past the Wallaby defence on a couple of occasions and was instrumental in helping O'Driscoll score that marvellous try.

It's a shame that Jeremy Davidson, a Lion in 1997, could not have been there to join the celebrations, but he wasn't far away anyway.

Davidson contemplated on the win. "It would have been nice to be in the team but it was still great to enjoy the achievement. We didn't expect a win like that and all the Irish guys did the business."

Wallaby coach Rod Macqueen was stunned. He and just about every serious rugby coach in Australia felt confident going into this Test.

"Yes, they took us a bit by surprise. I have to hold my hands up and say they were the better side. We just didn't play because we weren't allowed to play.

"It was uncharacteristic for us but Brian O'Driscoll and Rob Henderson cut us in shreds up the middle of the park. We can only hope to be able to answer that later in the series.

"It didn't help that Stephen Larkham missed a couple of tackles. That put a bit more pressure on the midfielders"

The Lions moaned rather than roared that referee Andre Watson appeared to penalise them off the pitch in the closing quarter but accepted later that he was probably right.

Reduced to 14 men for most of those last 20 minutes - Martin Corry and Phil Vickery were both shown yellow cards - it was inevitable that Australia would strike back from a 29-3 deficit. Still, while the Wallabies did their best, the Lions cover defence was superb. Phil Larder, employed to organise that defence, obviously did a superb job.

Australian fans could hardly believe what went on. They came into this game as firm favourites and were left to reflect on their future.

The Lions support was absolutely incredible and the stands were a sea of red with just the odd gold jersey visible.

It was like playing at home for these Lions and captain Martin Johnson acknowledged that with the following comments:

"During the warm up, I took one look and said to the boys, hey, it's like being on home soil. We can't let this opportunity go."

After establishing a 12-3 lead at the interval, and it should have been more, the Lions cut loose in the third quarter. Thanks to tries by O'Driscoll (what a memory) and Scott Quinnell, they burst into a 29-3 unassailable lead. From there on, Australia played catch-up rugby and only managed it in limited fashion when the Lions were reduced in numbers.

It was a fantastic win, the best I have ever witnessed on my fourth Lions tour.

SCORING SEQUENCE
FIRST HALF

3 mins - Jason Robinson try. 5-0.

21 mins - Andrew Walker penalty. 5-3

40 mins - Daffyd James try, Wilkinson conversion. 12-3.

SECOND HALF

2 mins - Brian O'Driscoll try, Wilkinson conversion. 19-3.

6 mins - Wilkinson penalty. 22-3.

12 mins - Scott Quinnell try, Wilkinson conversion. 29-3.

36 mins - Andrew Walker try. 29-8.

39 mins - Nathan Gray try. 29-13.

AUSTRALIA: C. Latham (Queensland), A. Walker (ACT), D. Herbert (Queensland), N. Gray (New South Wales), J. Roff (ACT), S. Larkham (ACT), G. Gregan (ACT), N. Stiles (Queensland), J. Paul (ACT), G. Panaho (New South Wales), G. Giffin (ACT), O.Finegan (ACT), T. Kefu (Queensland), G. Smith (ACT). Replacements. M. Burke (New South Wales) for Latham (half time), M. Foley (Queensland) for J. Paul (55), E. Flatley (Queensland) for Larkham (57), B. Darwin (ACT) for Panaho (68), M. Cockbain (Queensland) for Eales (78), D. Lyons (New South Wales) for Finegan (80).

BRITISH AND IRISH LIONS: M. Perry (England), D. James (Wales), B. O'Driscoll 9Ireland), R. Henderson (Ireland), J. Robinson (England), J. Wilkinson (England), R. Howley (Wales), T. Smith (Scotland0, K. Wood (Ireland), P. Vickery (England), M. Johnson (England), D. Grewcock (England), M. Corry (England), S. Quinnell (Wales), R. Hill (England). Replacements. I. Balshaw

(England) for Perry (half time), C. Charvis for Quinnell (70). Temporary replacement. G. Bulloch for Wood (75-79)

Referee. A. Watson (South Africa)

Lions record against Australia (First Tests)
1899: The Lions 3 Australia 11
1904: The Lions 17 Australia 0
1930: The Lions 5 Australia 6
1950: The Lions 19 Australia 6
1959: The Lions 17 Australia 6
1966: The Lions 11 Australia 8
1989: The Lions 12 Australia 30
2001: The Lions 29 Australia 13

Jeremy Davidson waves to the fans as he relaxes by the pool with Ronan O'Gara

David Wallace bursts away against ACT

251

Manager Donal Lenihan in happy mood at training after the Lions won the first Test

Tyrone Howe and Malcolm O'Kelly relax on the set of Australian Soap Opera Neighbours

Howe in full flight against New South Wales Country

CHAPTER 21

LAST GASP VICTORY

CANBERRA is hardly the liveliest place in the world. It's not a natural Capital, more manufactured to appease the people of Sydney and Melbourne. In winter it's usually a cold, damp place but, happily, the Lions visit coincided with reasonably good weather, bright sunny skies during the day and sharp, fresh conditions after dusk.

They say that Canberra has more Brothels than any other city in Australia and there are no ladies of the night on the streets. The image to be portrayed is that it is squeaky clean, but behind closed doors politicians and diplomats from all over the world must be having some kind of fun.

During their stay, the Lions certainly didn't because it was business as usual - on the training ground.

While the team to play ACT went out and did the business on the pitch, the Test side was preparing quietly for the second game against the Wallabies and for the golden opportunity to wrap up the Test series.

Four key ACT players hoped to make a lasting impression and push their claims for a place in the series.

Centres Graeme Bond and James Holbeck, out half Pat Howard and second row Justin Harrison all harboured hopes of elevation.

Bond and Holbeck in the backs and Harrison had seriously good games for Australia A against the tourists while Howard, last year's European Player of the Year when helping Leicester to Heineken Cup victory, was back at base attempting to stake a claim.

Whatever about the future, none of the four made it in their own right although Harrison started the third Test as a replacement for the injured David Giffin. For both sides, ACT and the Wallabies, he made a lasting impression and monumental contributions.

Prior to the game, Lions coach Graham Henry spoke of total respect for a team that has achieved so much in the last three seasons.

Twice Super 12 runners-up, they finally hit the glory trail at the third attempt. In the words of Wallaby vice-captain George Gregan: "We did it the hard way but we never lost sight of what we were capable of even after losing two finals."

Gregan, of course, was on duty with Australia and therefore not available to lead his side. Even with eight regulars, ACT proved they have come a long way since 1989 when the Lions, after a struggle, managed to pull away for a 41-25 victory.

This was very much a second string Lions side. Iain Balshaw was given another chance to press for a place in the team for the second Test but didn't take that opportunity, while the only others in close contention were Austin Healey and Matt Dawson, both of whom were ultimately selected in the replacements, although Healey later withdrew because of injury.

Anyone else with designs on a Test place really didn't have a prayer given the circumstances that prevailed before the Lions ran away with a lucky win.

Match 8: Australian Capital Territories
Bruce Stadium, Canberra, July 3.
Attendance: 20,093. Weather: Cold, dry. Pitch: Soft.
ACT BRUMBIES 28 (M. Bartholomeausz, W. Gordon, D. Tuiavii try each, T. Hall 3 penalties, 2 conversions) BRITISH AND IRISH LIONS 30 (A. Healey 2 tries, D. Wallace try, M. Dawson 3 penalties, 3 conversions)

NEW Wallaby coach Eddie Jones came to within an ace of plotting the downfall of the British and Irish Lions for the second time on tour.

But there was an ironic twist to this match when two of the most controversial characters in the Lions party combined to deny the Super 12 champions the result they probably deserved.

Austin Healey scored the last minute try and Matt Dawson converted to leave the Brumbies well and truly shattered at the end of an energy-sapping contest.

It was an emotional occasion for both Jones and star back rower Jim Williams, both of whom were involved with the squad for the last time.

Williams broke a bone in his hand and was forced to go to hospital for treatment shortly after the finish. Jones admitted, "I gave him a big hug before he left. We won't see one another for some time. He has served the Brumbies well and I have no doubt that he will make a big impact in Ireland with Munster."

The game itself, from the Lions point of view, could best be described as an escape from jail.

They hardly deserved the win and it was ironic that Matt Dawson, who had slagged off the training methods endorsed by coach Graham Henry earlier in the week, was the one who came to their rescue with that last second conversion of Healey's try.

In fairness to Dawson, he kept a steady nerve and the additional points, as well as the victory, were secured from the time the ball was kicked.

The fact that Dawson had been given the goal-kicking duties ahead of Ronan O'Gara raised a few eyebrows and left the Irish international somewhat disillusioned.

It was clear from Henry's decision that O'Gara would take no part in the Test series although, because of injury, he was named in the squad of 22 for the final Test in Sydney.

Some of Henry's thinking confused a lot of people when one considers was happened five days later.

"We wanted Dawson put under pressure to see what he was made of." The Northampton player could not be accused of letting the Lions down in this particular game yet Neil Jenkins was named as a reserve for the second Test and Henry admitted that he would be back-up goal kicker to Jonny Wilkinson if the English star picked up an injury. Very strange given the circumstances of the Lions victory over ACT.

As it transpired, Jenkins did make a late appearance in that second Test when Wilkinson was carried off but he never got an opportunity to kick for goal. Even if he had, it wouldn't have mattered as Australia had already secured a comprehensive victory by the time he came on the pitch.

Pity O'Gara. The Irishman was given little opportunity to press for a Test place. Wilkinson was always the first choice out-half but the Cork man was justifiably aggrieved that he had not been given a real chance to edge in as number two, particularly when one considers the slump in form suffered by Jenkins.

He did everything possible in this game to give himself a chance with some excellent line kicking and a couple of sniping runs, one of which led directly to a crucial try scored by David Wallace.

ACT, with only two players from their first choice team, can feel they did themselves proud in the circumstances.

The Lions may have escaped with a last gasp victory but they really were lucky.

Having said that, their match-winning try and conversion was brilliantly created and executed to perfection. They went through six passages of play as the clock counted down and Healey never lost sight of the target once he got the scoring chance.

ACT raced into a 14-0 lead with an explosion of brilliant play that left the Lions reeling. Bond carved up the midfield defence alongside Holbeck while out half Pat Howard was involved in many assisted moves.

The Lions had a couple of scoring chances in that opening half but were lucky not to trail by more than 10-22 at the interval. Ronan O'Gara and Scott Gibbs came closest to making the break-through with bursts in the 32nd and 37th minute. Apart from that, and an interception try from Healey, inspiration from the visiting side was sadly lacking.

The Lions did well for long spells in the second half but continued to be outplayed by their local rivals.

ACT are a very good side and obviously well versed in the art of slowing play down.

They went on to establish a 28-23 lead going into injury time and obviously forgot that they should have used every means at their disposal to keep the scoreline in their favour.

The Lions, in their desperation, threw everything they could at ACT in the final minutes. The seconds were counting down but they built up to six phases of play. Ruck to ruck, maul to maul, out to the backs and, finally, Healey skipped in for the try that levelled the match before Dawson knocked over the conversion to give the Lions an unexpected victory.

From an Irish point of view, O'Gara, David Wallace and Jeremy Davidson did well in difficult circumstances. It was to be their last appearance on the tour but they did themselves proud in the circumstances that prevailed ... a crowded itinerary that really allowed little scope to shine, especially when Henry appeared to have his mind made up from day one.

SCORING SEQUENCE
FIRST HALF

7 mins - Mark Bartholomeausz try. Travis Hall conversion. 7-0.

12 mins - Willie Gordon try, Hall conversion. 14-0.

19 mins - Matt Dawson penalty. 14-3.

25 mins - Des Tuiavii try. 19-3.

37 mins - Austin Healey try. Matt Dawson conversion. 19-10.

39 mins - Hall penalty. 22-10.

SECOND HALF

3 mins- David Wallace try, Dawson conversion. 22-17.

17 mins - Dawson penalty. 22-20.

25 mins - Hall penalty. 25-22.

35 mins - Dawson penalty. 25-23.

40 mins - Hall penalty. 28-23.

47 mins - Austin Healey try, Dawson conversion. 30-28 to Lions.

ACT BRUMBIES: M. Bartholomeusz, D. McInally, G. Bond, J. Holbeck, W. Gordon, P. Howard, T. Hall, A. Scott, A. Freier, M. Weaver, J. Harrison, D. Vickerman, P. Ryan, J. Williams (captain), D. Tuiavii. Replacements. D. Pusey for Williams (55), C. Pither for Gordon (75).

BRITISH AND IRISH LIONS: I. Balshaw(England), B. Cohen (England), M. Taylor (Wales), S. Gibbs (Wales), A. Healey (England), R. O'Gara (Ireland), M. Dawson (England), D. Morris (Wales), D. West (England), D. Young (Wales) captain; J. Davidson (Ireland), S. Murray (Scotland), D. Wallace (Ireland), M. Corry (England), M. Williams (Wales). Replacements. J. Leonard (England) for Young (75). Temporary replacement. D. James (Wales) for Williams (17-22).

259

Referee. P. Marshall (New South Wales).

Lions record against ACT
1989: The Lions 41 ACT 25
2001: The Lions 30 ACT 28

CHAPTER 22

BACK TO SQUARE ONE

THE days leading up to the second Test were filled with controversial remarks on both sides of the divide.

Wallaby captain John Eales came under pressure amidst suggestions that he might well have been dropped for the game.

Former great Michael Lynagh remarked: "I feel the Lions are happy to see an under-prepared, injured and distracted Eales playing rather than Justin Harrison, who cut a swathe through the tourists in the Australia A match earlier in the tour."

Lynagh didn't stop there. He also criticised Stephen Larkham when he said: "His form has been strangely lacklustre of late. He has started to fall off tackles, get caught with the ball and generally doesn't seem enthusiastic about playing."

Larkham jumped to Eales' defence but admitted the tactics Australia brought into the first match were all wrong and that the side was, as suggested, complacent.

He admitted his own form was not up to scratch but was none too pleased with the timing of Lynagh's remarks either.

"You don't become a bad player and a team doesn't become a bad team on the basis of one performance. I think he took the criticism a little bit too far. A few of the players have spoken to him

261

about it and suggested that these remarks are not helpful to anyone involved with the Australian team.

"I'm not that worried about what he said because there is an element of truth in the remarks. If you have a bad game, there's not very much you can do about it except get up, dust yourself down and face into the next match hoping that everything will be all right."

Larkham's revelations of the preparation and mood in the Australian camp in the lead-up to the Gabba disaster were in contrast to coach Rod Mccqueen's view that the team had never been more motivated.

"We were probably ambushed. We weren't expecting to see so many Lions supporters for a start and we didn't expect the Lions were capable of playing as well as they did. Our attitude going into the game was obviously wrong."

Former coach Bob Dwyer, who led the Wallabies to their 1991 World Cup success, also made that point.

"People often ask me before a game whether the guys are switched on. My experience has taught me to reply: 'I'll let you know midway through the second half' because there is no way you can get inside a guy's head during training and preparation. In the first game, I sensed something was wrong early on. After running onto the pitch, one of the players was laughing with a teammate. During the National Anthem, another player actually winked at a TV camera.

"Both of those things can be signs of nerves, but laughing and joking is – at worst – a manifestation of a far too relaxed attitude."

Larkham also suggested the Wallaby tactics were not good on the day. "We went out with the intention of spinning the ball wide and hoping to catch their defensive weakness out there. Neither I nor the rest of the team were therefore allowed to really get into the game.

"I also made a tactical error of wearing moulded boots that were fine except when play was centred around the cricket pitch area. Once I hit that, my boots just clogged up with mud and I had absolutely no traction."

Meanwhile, in the Lions camp there was more unrest. Criticism of the Lions training schedule brought a stinging rebuke from management and players alike. Dawson, at least, had the guts to stand up and apologise for the timing of his remarks, if not for his viewpoint that the players had been flogged to death by coach Henry on the training ground.

Austin Healey appeared to take no notice of management's plea for unity because he quickly jumped on the bandwagon and went much further than Dawson.

Healey, nicknamed "motor mouth" by the Australian media, claimed Henry had no real influence in plotting the downfall of the Wallabies in the first Test.

He claimed the tourists moved away from Henry's game plan when they made an early strike against Australia with a try to Jason Robinson.

He wrote in an English newspaper: "I know you are still waiting for me to get to the game-plan, waiting for me to say what went right and wrong. Well, I can't, except to say getting the ball to Jason in the second minute was definitely not in the script.

"I bet you think he (Henry) was upset because the lads had broken a rule by passing the ball to Jason. Well, no. He had a grin the size of whatever is very, very big. That came as a bit of a shock. The grin, that is. Haven't seen him do that too often!"

While Healey remained defiant in his criticism for the remainder of the tour, Dawson admitted a sense of guilt about what he had said.

"I was disappointed at myself for taking the gloss off what had been a fantastic achievement (the first Test win) for all concerned. I let myself down, but more importantly I let the squad down.

"There were things mentioned in my diary that should have remained confidential. I put in jeopardy the trust and confidence that had built up within the whole group.

263

"That means a lot to me. What makes me really tick is the sense of being part of a group. I like to be liked and I like to give my all for those around me. That was put under strain and I'm disappointed it came to that."

It is believed that team manager Donal Lenihan's initial reaction was to banish Dawson from the tour but was advised against it by Syd Millar, chairman of the Four Home Unions. That stance by Lenihan was never confirmed. Neither were details of the punishment made public but it is known that he was heavily fined and warned of his future conduct.

It was clear, though, that Dawson was forgiven following the initial storming reaction from Lenihan and the reaction from his colleagues.

Captain Martin Johnson apparently pleaded for leniency for one of the heroes of the 1997 series win over South Africa.

"Matt can't believe he wrote what he did. He is very upset by the whole affair and is desperate to put things right. I can sympathise with him in a way because it has been a very tough tour. The squad has made peace with him and Matt has made peace with the squad. Now we just want to move on," said Johnson.

History was made in this second Test. The Lions had only ever played Australia in either Sydney or Brisbane. The ARU is making a concerted effort to spread interest in the game outside these traditional strongholds of Rugby Union. Already, of course, the ARU has been successful in the creation of a third rugby state, ACT, and are anxious to heighten interest in the AFL domain of Melbourne.

Although Australian Rules actually does rule in Melbourne, the decision proved to be inspirational and the game was a sell out only hours after tickets had gone on sale two months before.

The weather was not part of the equation because the ARU decreed the roof on the stadium would be closed for the match.

The Lions management were not keen on that, somehow believing Australia would be provided with an unfair advantage.

How they came to that conclusion is anybody's guess but the decision, following discussions with Four Home Unions Chairman Syd Millar, stood and the atmosphere, let it be said, was electric.

Millar, displaying his usual sense of humour, was alleged to have told ARU Chief Executive John O'Neill that he would agree to close the roof on one condition – that it would be opened if the Lions were trailing at half time.

O'Neill readily agreed but pointed out that the roof actually takes 40 minutes to fully retract!

Match 9: Australia (Second Test)
Colonial Stadium, Melbourne, July 7.
Attendance: 58,215. Weather: Dry. Pitch: Firm (played under closed roof).

AUSTRALIA 35 (M. Burke try, 6 penalties, conversion, J. Roff 2 tries) BRITISH AND IRISH LIONS 14 (N. Back try, J. Wilkinson 2 penalties)

GRAHAM HENRY'S perception that the British and Irish Lions won three of the four halves during the opening two Test games may well be valid but the facts remain, after this second Test, that the series was all square going into the decider in Sydney.

The Lions won the first half 11-6 and lost the second 29-3. That told a sad story of this amazing game played indoors.

Henry came under mounting pressure after his team allowed a major first half advantage slip away. The ball went back to the Wallaby court and coach Rod Macqueen was given the perfect opportunity to retire from the job with more success under his belt.

Few believed Macqueen when he said he had announced his early retirement to the players AFTER the game.

It must surely have been mentioned at half time because, clearly, in the second half these Wallabies appeared prepared to do anything to secure a glorious exit for their much beloved coach.

Macqueen had intended to retire and give way to Eddie Jones, the ACT Brumbies coach, in September after the Tri-Nations tournament. He changed his mind and that surely was a motivating factor for the players - who must have known.

The outcome was also probably a case of the inevitable to mark the occasion of a milestone for John Eales, the Wallaby captain.

The Wallabies were stretched to the limit in the first half but showed grim determination. The half-time team talk had to have something to do with the amazing turnabout. That, a little bit of luck and some downright appalling errors from the Lions.

Nobody could have predicted the record margin of victory at the Colonial Stadium based on the respective performances in the first Test a week before.

The British and Irish Lions suffered as much in defence as in attack, and they collapsed completely after conceding a try 30 seconds into the second period.

The Lions left this game behind them in the first half when they had the Wallabies on the rack for much of the period.

A succession of turnovers allied to the inability to win clean line out possession was crucial to the problems they encountered. Instead of being ahead by 20 points, and they would have deserved that, they were up by just five.

After Joe Roff scored a brilliant try, albeit following a stupid mistake by Jonny Wilkinson, the game was up, all over, cut and dried. And that was a try which only brought the world champions level!

What happened later brought them to heady heights, to a record victory over the Lions and, more importantly, to a levelling of the series. It probably saved Rod Macqueen, the Wallaby coach, from being asked to leave the post before his September deadline, but he had made the decision anyway.

For Eales, in his 50th game as Australian captain and Daniel Herbert, winning his 50th cap, it was a night to remember.

The advantage now goes back to Australia in a bigger stadium where the Lions supporters will be much less conspicuous.

Eales, however, was not convinced of automatic victory. "I reckon the Lions made a lot of mistakes and didn't put us away when they might have in the first half.

"They did not take their scoring opportunities and we did at crucial periods of the second half.

"We lost the plot in the first match. They lost it in the second but I still don't believe there is much between the sides.

"This Lions team is extremely dangerous. Next week's game has its own entity and will be decided probably by a couple of things that go wrong or right for one side or the other," he said at the time and was proven right in his assessment.

"We knew we had to improve from the first game and I figure we did that. But we got a couple of tries because the Lions made mistakes rather than due to our own expertise. Take those points off the score and there was never much between us. Thankfully, the tries came at good times for us and it clearly unsettled them."

His Lions counterpart Martin Johnson accepted that the touring side probably blew it. "In the modern game, one or two errors can be disastrous. The game moves away from you and you try to push things a bit more. That can often lead to more mistakes and it is all over before you can blink."

Johnson and Henry both agreed that the following days would have to be spent working on the psychological as much as the physical.

"We have got to persuade people that that game was there for the taking; that we were good enough to win it and that we beat the Wallabies once so there is no reason it can't be done twice," said Johnson.

"It was always going to be difficult and I always believed this series would go down to the wire. It would be nice if I was able to sit here and reflect on a series win but I can't. Yet, we have everything to play for still. We beat South Africa four years ago and I have every confidence we are capable of beating Australia.

"Nobody ever suggested this tour would be easy. They are the world champions and they didn't win the title easily. We know what we have to do - and that is to play brilliantly, but I believe we are capable of doing so."

Sadly, John's aspirations did not materialise.

SCORING SEQUENCE
FIRST HALF

7 mins - Jonny Wilkinson penalty. 3-0.

11 mins - Wilkinson penalty. 6-0.

18 mins - Matt Burke penalty. 6-3.

27 mins - Neil Back try. 11-3.

40 mins - Burke penalty. 11-6.

SECOND HALF

30 seconds - Joe Roff try. 11-11.

5 mins - Burke penalty. 14-11

9 mins - Roff try, Burke conversion. 21-11.

18 mins - J. Wilkinson penalty. 21-14.

25 mins - Burke try. 26-14.

33 mins - Burke penalty. 29-14.

42 mins - Burke penalty. 32-14.

47 mins - Burke penalty. 35.14.

AUSTRALIA: M. Burke (New South Wales), A. Walker (ACT), D. Herbert (Queensland), N. Gray (New South Wales), J. Roff (ACT), S. Larkham (ACT), G. Gregan (ACT), N. Stiles (Queensland), M. Foley (Queensland), R. Moore (New South Wales), D. Giffin (ACT), J. Eales (Queensland) captain: O. Finegan

(ACT), T. Kefu (Queensland), G. Smith (ACT). Replacements. C. Latham (Queensland) for Walker (46), E. Flatley (Queensland) for Larkham (82), M. Cockbain (Queensland) for Giffin (83), B. Cannon (New South Wales) for Foley (86).

BRITISH AND IRISH LIONS: M. Perry (England), D. James (Wales), B. O'Driscoll (Ireland), R. Henderson (Ireland), J. Robinson (England), J. Wilkinson (England), R. Howley (Wales), T. Smith (Scotland), K. Wood (Ireland), P. Vickery (England), M. Johnson (England) captain; D. Grewcock (England), R. Hill (England), S. Quinnell (Wales), N. Back (England). Replacements: M. Corry (England) for Hill (half time), I. Balshaw (England) for Perry (53), J. Leonard (England) for Vickery (62), N. Jenkins (Wales) for Wilkinson (73) M. Dawson (England) for Howley (82)

Referee. J. Kaplan (South Africa)

Lions record against Australia (Second Tests)
1899: The Lions 11 Australia 0
1904: The Lions 17 Australia 3
1950: The Lions 24 Australia 3
1959: The Lions 24 Australia 3
1966: The Lions 31 Australia 0
1989: The Lions 19 Australia 12
2001: The Lions 14 Australia 35.

CHAPTER 23

BROKEN HEARTS

THE war of words continued, almost interrupted, in the week leading up to the final Test at Stadium Australia.

Occasionally, the headlines switched from stinging criticism on both sides to stories of injuries in both camps.

Wallaby play-maker Stephen Larkham and second row David Giffin struggled to overcome injuries during that week but coach Rod Macqueen gave them every chance to prove themselves.

Richard Hill was ruled out for the Lions with concussion but Jonny Wilkinson, carried off late in the second Test, was said to be making progress. Speculation on all three gave us something else to write about.

Because both sides trained mostly behind closed doors, and many miles apart at that, it was difficult to assess whether it was bluff, fact or fiction.

On another front, the Lions and Australian management teams kept bashing away at one another with accusations and counter-accusations.

Rod Macqueen charged that Larkham, who was ultimately ruled out with a damaged shoulder, was hit late three times in the second Test. "We are disappointed with some of the things that happened him but we have opted not to talk about it at this stage," said the coach.

Lions defensive coach Phil Larder admitted that Larkham had been targeted but insisted it had been legal and all above board.

"The more times Steve Larkham is on the floor the better … but there was never anything malicious or unfair about it. It's a physical game and tackling the opposition is a major part of it."

Manager Donal Lenihan added: "Larkham has been carrying an injury into the Test series so I don't think his problem can be put down to us. There were two late tackles that I can remember but I don't think they were in any way malicious. There was never any notion by us to go and take him out of the game. As for tackling him out of it and upsetting him, that's all part of rugby."

Lions coach Graham Henry added: "It's been clear he has struggled with injury. Quite honestly, we were hoping he would play in the third Test unfit as well."

In the circumstances, Lenihan saw the need to hit back and he did in a vigorous manner when calling for the suspension of Wallaby centre Nathan Gray.

English flanker Richard Hill, a key figure for the Lions, lost the opportunity to play in the deciding match after Gray elbowed him in the head 37 minutes into the second game.

It was an off the ball incident and Lenihan insisted the centre should have been cited by commissioner David Gray from New Zealand.

"We had a good look at the video and were very unhappy with the way Richard was injured. The whole citing procedure is well known and we contacted the commissioner to say we wanted action. I got a call subsequently to say there was no reason why action should be taken and that was the end of the matter.

"I am unhappy that there is no procedure for an appeal. We were told that he (David Gray) did not have to offer an explanation. He just gave a ruling and that's it. I am very disappointed because it has knocked one of our best players out of the Test series.

"One of our players, Colin Charvis, was suspended for dropping a knee on the back of a player. That incident, in relation to this, was far less serious. Colin Charvis was cited; we took our punishment, and in my view there should have been similar action in this instance. You cannot even compare the two. The player injured after the Charvis incident got up and played on. Unfortunately, Richard Hill was unable to finish the tour."

Early in the week, the Lions named a squad of 27 players as they struggled with injuries.

Amongst that group was Irish flanker and replacement player David Wallace. He got a brief thrill because 24 hours later, with fitness issues more or less sorted out, he was back with the midweek men and off the tour. It was time to party instead of preparing for a Test match.

The decision to exclude Wallace came as a surprise to former English prop Jeff Probyn who made a big case for the Garryowen player.

In fact, Probyn took issue with Graham Henry on a number of counts. He suggested that Dai Young be picked before Phil Vickery and either Ronan O'Gara or Austin Healey before Wilkinson.

"One of the problems in the second Test was scrummaging. If you can't have a solid scrum, and the Lions didn't, then you are in trouble. Young would have had enough gas in the tank to last 60 minutes and could have done enough damage by then.

"Jonny Wilkinson is a gifted player in many ways and a great defender. The trouble is he doesn't have enough gas. He will make a break but defenders know they will always catch him.

"Healey is unpredictable and capable of unlocking the best defences while O'Gara has more pace as well. Maybe he (O'Gara) is still a bit raw but he has a lot going for him, not least the fact that he is a fantastic distributor of the ball. I don't think he gets enough credit for the space he creates for others."

As for Wallace, Probyn believed he would have made his mark had he been called into the squad just a little earlier.

"The ideal back row would have been Martin Corry, Scott Quinnell and Richard Hill, but with Hill out that wasn't possible. I think the selectors made a mistake by changing it around for the second Test when Neil Back became available.

"Now, with Hill out, I would certainly have gone for Wallace. He had a fine game against ACT and games don't come much bigger than that. He got his body in the way and that is something that Neil Back didn't do in the second Test.

"The Lions needed someone whose game had not been studied in depth by the Australians and Wallace was the perfect example of that. He was outstanding against ACT, his mobility was equal to anyone else in the party.

"Guys have to be given a chance and I don't go with the theory that players originally selected should always get first shot. Martin Corry is a case in point. He went to Australia at short notice and you would have to admire the way he responded to the challenge. It just shows that selectors can be wrong. When they are, they should admit it and do what is right. In this case, Wallace should have been chosen ahead of Back."

"I hope I am wrong and that the guys selected, Back included, go out there and do the business. I'm just a bit worried they won't."

The result will show that Probyn was spot on.

AUSTRALIA 29 (D. Herbert 2 tries, M. Burke 5 penalties, 2 conversions) BRITISH AND IRISH LIONS 23 (J. Wilkinson try, 3 penalties, 2 conversions, J. Robinson try)

THE course of history was changed for the first time in over one hundred years when the British and Irish Lions lost their first Test series in Australia on a whim in Sydney.

A glaring lack of ability out of touch, the grave tendency to allow Australia steal their lineout ball, cost the 2001 Lions this game and the series.

No wonder then that Martin Johnson, the tall senior figure of this Lions party should look so glum.

He had every reason to be. Earlier in the tour, his English partners Matt Dawson and Austin Healey let the side down. On Saturday, Johnson did the same.

He lost possession on the Wallaby line in the closing stages when rookie second row Justin Harrison snaffled a Lions throw, perfectly aimed to Johnson by Keith Wood.

It was the defining moment of a very close match.

But, of course, it wasn't the first time. Either Wood was throwing badly or Johnson called badly. The Lions lost four of their own throws. That either says something about Johnson or his main opponent Harrison, but there is no doubt that the lineout calls were poor.

The Lions lost one on their own line and another on the Australian line - both at crucial times of the game.

Coaches talk about the merit of finding men at the back because, they say, the team in possession have more attacking options. My view is that you must secure possession before you can attack. The safe option is to throw to two and secure that possession. A team cannot play without the ball and the Lions blew the chance to secure possession on two very crucial stages of the game.

Ironically, though, it was that last short throw that probably cost them the match because the competitive Harrison went against his captain's advice and attacked Johnson in a successful bid to rob him of possession.

All credit to Australia. The world champions looked bedraggled after the first Test, hit back to win the second and then, in a very close encounter, had the nerve to pull away at the end.

It was a fantastic series with each team scoring the exact same number of tries in three games. But the Wallabies are winners and they showed exactly why they are at Stadium Australia.

Lions coach Graham Henry headed off to New Zealand on the Monday after the game to reflect on a job that was unfinished. "We left ourselves down at the end of the day. We had the chance to take the series but the Wallabies proved themselves to be a very good team. You have got to take your hat off to them."

At least, the Lions did not disgrace themselves. It could have been worse after losing to the Wallabies in the second Test.

"I am not in the mood for making any excuses but we were not able to put our best team or not able to prepare the team properly in the lead up to the game.

"The starting XV didn't have more than one full training session together. Some of the guys out there were strapped together. In that sense, I am very proud of them. They showed character and skill and eventually lost to what was, quite simply, a better side."

In front of 85,000 people at a stadium that could have taken 20 per cent more, The Lions supporters did themselves proud. The colour gold may have been more obvious but the men and women in red made more noise throughout the evening. It was agonisingly close and the game was only decided in the closing ten minutes when Matthew Burke knocked over a couple of penalties to clinch the series and the Tom Richards trophy, ironically paid for by Irishman Tony O'Reilly, though the Heinz company.

It was a remarkable night at Stadium Australia and a great farewell to Wallaby coach Rod Macqueen.

Eddie Jones took over the squad afterwards prepare for the Tri-Nations Championship and the next World Cup, but this was Macqueen's great moment.

Under pressure a fortnight ago, captain John Eales and Macqueen huddled together, hugged and embraced at the end of this absorbing tussle. Australia has always had to fight hard for success on a rugby pitch. Victory over the Lions for the first time in 102 years, will give the sport a massive shot in the arm.

It has been conceded that the Lions, despite their defeat, have been a decent touring side. Former Queensland coach John Connolly went so far as to say: "The Lions had the better of four of the six halves in the three Tests. But they lost, and that came down to sheer grit on the part of the Australians. This tour will be remembered as a war of attrition. The Lions had many heroes but Australia just happened to have more."

That was never so apparent when Daniel Herbert was shown the yellow card in the first half for a desperately high tackle on Brian O'Driscoll.

Sensing that they had the world champions on the rack, the Lions proceeded to self-destruct and the Wallabies dug deep to keep the ball away from the visitors and then defend as is their lives depended on it. By the time Herbert came back, all the Lions had to show for their efforts were three points.

The battle raged throughout the opening half with the teams scoring a try apiece. The Wallabies edged in front and held a 16-13 lead at the break before Jonny Wilkinson scorched over for an early second half try. Eleven minutes into that period, the teams were level and it stayed that way until the closing minutes when Matt Burke struck two penalties.

The most important moment of the match, however, came in the last minute when the Lions won a throw a yard from the Wallaby line. The rolling maul they perfected on the tour was just waiting to be used but a team needs the ball to execute it. Sadly for the Lions, and happily for the Wallabies, rookie Harrison intervened and the chance was lost.

They came that close … but not close enough.

SCORING SEQUENCE
FIRST HALF

2 mins - Matthew Burke penalty. 3-0.

6 mins - Jonny Wilkinson penalty. 3-3.

12 mins - Burke penalty. 6-3.

16 mins - Burke penalty. 9-3.

20 mins - Jason Robinson try, Wilkinson conversion. 10-9.

42 mins - Daniel Herbert try, Burke conversion. 16-10.

44 mins - Wilkinson penalty. 16-13.

SECOND HALF

2 mins - Wilkinson try, conversion. 20-16.

10 mins - Herbert try, Burke conversion. 23-20.

11 mins - Wilkinson penalty. 23-23.

29 mins - Burke penalty. 26-23.

39 mins - Burke penalty. 29-23.

AUSTRALIA: M. Burke (New South Wales),A. Walker (ACT), D. Herbert (Queensland), N. Gray (New South Wales), J. Roff (ACT), E. Flatley (Queensland), G. Gregan (ACT), N. Stiles (Queensland), M. Foley (New South Wales), R. Moore (ACT), J. Harrison (ACT), J. Eales (Queensland) captain; O. Finegan (ACT), T. Kefu (Queensland), G. Smith (ACT). Replacements. M. Cockbain for Finegan (67).

BRITISH AND IRISH LIONS: M. Perry (England), D. James (Wales), B. O'Driscoll (Ireland), R. Henderson (Ireland), J. Robinson (England), J. Wilkinson (England), M. Dawson (England), T. Smith (Scotland), K. Wood (Ireland), P. Vickery (England), M. Johnson (England) captain; D. Grewcock (England), M. Corry (England), S. Quinnell (Wales), N. Back (England).

Replacements. C. Charvis (Wales) for Quinnell (half time), I. Balshaw (England) for James, D. Morris (Wales) for Smith (both 73).

Referee. P. O'Brien (New Zealand).

Lions record against Australia (Third Tests).
1899: The Lions 11 Australia 10
1904: The Lions 16 Austalia 0
1989: The Lions 19 Australia 18
2001: The Lions 23 Australia 29

Note: Fourth Test
1899: The Lions 13 Australia 0

CHAPTER 24

NOTHING AT THE
END OF THE RAINBOW

THE look of utter dejection on the face of Keith Wood summed up the feeling of the entire squad.

Wood had not even considered defeat in the third Test when he declared: "We will reach our potential and when we do we will win this game. I'm not burying my head in the sand. I believe we have the quality in the side to win this series."

The comments were made in Manly on the Thursday before the big deciding match at Stadium Australia.

Wood was angry that the Lions had let the chance of glory slip the week before and was determined to complete a second memorable Test series victory over the reigning World Champions.

Wood had been party to a stirring triumph in South Africa in 1997 and saw no reason why the Lions couldn't enhance the reputation of rugby in the northern hemisphere by doing it again.

In the end, Wood and his colleagues had to settle for second best. Two late penalties from Matt Burke and failure to win a line-out in the last minute of the match were the key aspects of the Australian victory, a victory snatched from the jaws of defeat.

With the details of the 2001 tour now consigned to the history books, the only things to remain are memories. For everyone involved, those memories were mixed between the good and the bad.

Things have changed on Lions tours since the game became professional. In the old days, the press corps was almost as much a part of the "Circus" as the players. Not any more.

The management of this Lions tour was single minded in what they wanted to achieve from it and it was hard to level blame at anyone for that. Every Lions tour is judged on results and this Lions tour was different and more intense than any other.

Ten matches crammed into six weeks didn't give the squad much time to prepare or the management much time to prepare themselves. The hard work had to start immediately.

Unfortunately, there were communication problems from the start, and the press sometimes appeared to be in an exclusion zone.

The timing of press conferences was changed several times at short notice, sometimes they were held at a different venue from the one planned and requests to have specific players present were not always honoured. On "open days", some of the players appeared to be a law into themselves. If they decided to turn up they turned up, if they decided against it, they didn't.

Inevitably, that led to annoyance and there were times when the relationship between those on both sides of the divide was uneasy. Pity.

One of the difficulties may have been the fact that a number of the players were engaged by various newspapers throughout Britain and Ireland to write weekly columns.

In the case of Rob Henderson, who wrote for the Irish Examiner and Malcolm O'Kelly, who penned articles for the Irish Independent, it didn't seem to matter. They were available to anyone who wanted to talk to them and I'm sure there were others from different countries that adapted the same attitude.

Two or three players, at least, remained aloof. If they were not absolutely obstructive, they were certainly close to it even when they were obviously in the news and reaction to one thing or another was required.

Two players in particular, Matt Dawson and Austin Healey, landed themselves in hot water with hard-hitting critical comments of the management, particularly of Graham Henry's coaching methods.

These were enough to prompt manager Donal Lenihan to take immediate action against Dawson during the tour and demand that Healey also be taken to task after the party returned home.

It is Lenihan's view that the whole matter of writing newspaper articles spiralled out of control, but he concedes that nothing could be done about it because several players had agreed contracts before they signed anything with the Lions.

Lenihan wasn't in the slightest bit surprised by the fact that certain players moaned about training schedules and about the lack of free time they had at their disposal.

"In a sense, I would have to sympathise with them. When you have a squad of 37 people, it was obvious we could not keep them all happy all of the time. Players were disappointed at not being picked, but it was really no different to the previous tours I was involved in."

Lenihan was a player in New Zealand in 1983 and in Australia six years later. "I can recall players cribbing on both tours I was involved in. In New Zealand, people didn't like the intensity of some of the training sessions under Jim Telfer but we had to grin and bear it. In 1989 there were also some complaints and I know, having spoken to those involved in tours to New Zealand in 1993 and even South Africa four years ago, that things were just the same.

"The big difference was that we didn't get to read about it in the press because the players didn't go public, particularly while the tour was going on. I think most of the articles were fine but that one or two people over-stepped the mark and that will have to be examined closely for future reference. I just think it deflected away from the things the players should have been thinking about."

Indeed, a number of the English media, in their assessment of the tour were at one on this issue.

The Mail on Sunday representative concluded: "While it would be fatuous to blame Healey for inspiring an Australian victory, it served no purpose to his team in winding up an already wired opposition."

The Sunday Telegraph went further. Reacting to Healey's broadside attack on Australian second row Justin Harrison, the report said: "Healey's comments were as puerile as they were offensive and Harrison, in winning a number of important line-outs and restarts, exposed Healey for the fool that he is."

Sunday Times rugby man Stephen Jones said Healey's "nonsense" could not be divorced from Harrison's performance.

"How can we separate his towering debut from the ridiculing of him beforehand? What a pity Healey should be so disrespectful to an opposing player and so indifferent to his own team's performance."

Lenihan accepted this was the toughest tour to date in terms of free time, or lack of it. The days when the Lions were roving ambassadors for British and Irish rugby are well and truly over. There are no longer visits to local schools, no longer inter-action with local communities. These days, the Lions can only do their talking on the pitch and can only win friends by playing good rugby.

The manager accepted that a part of the thrill of touring had gone forever. "I would have liked to see the players have more free time and we did our best to make that time available to them.

"It wasn't always possible and it didn't help that the games were scheduled for evening time. On previous tours, the players would have finished their games at around 5 o'clock in the afternoon. On this one, they never got back to the hotel much before midnight and then had to face moving on early the following day. They didn't even have time to unwind after the matches."

Neither did the Lions have opportunities to unwind during the week and management, particularly coach Graham Henry, must shoulder blame for that.

There was no doubt that the talkative players, even those consigned to the midweek team, had some valid reasons to speak out.

The training sessions, many of them at any rate, were arduous and too long. Henry, it should be remembered, was only second choice to coach this Lions squad. Lenihan tried to move heaven and earth to persuade Ian McGeechan to come on board for the fourth time in his career. Two months of soft talking and several visits to Scotland were not enough.

Henry is a very different type of coach and has a very different personality. He didn't smile that often and struggled to win over the players, even some of the Welsh representatives.

We can all talk, we can speculate as to what might have happened had McGeechan taken the job. It may have been different. It may not.

One thing is for sure. He would have handled things differently. There would have been more free time and shorter, sharper training sessions geared to giving the players some sort of recovery period following an exhausting 11 month season.

He would have smiled a lot more with and at the players and press. He would have helped create a bit more fun within the party. That fun would not have been manufactured. It would have been spontaneous.

It is also likely that the players in the "exclusion" zone would have known exactly why they were there and whether they had any chance of getting out of it.

The lack of communication, the lack of explanation, was a damning indictment of Henry's short reign as Lions coaching Supremo. One doubts if he will be asked to coach them again.

In mitigation, he did have to plan without a number of key players injured either on the training "paddock" or on the pitch.

The Lions lost Phil Greening, Simon Taylor, Mike Catt, Dan Luger, Robin McBryde, Lawrence Dallaglio, all of whom had to return home and both Richard Hill and Rob Howley for the last Test.

Early in the week prior to that last game, no less than 18 of the tour party were receiving treatment for injuries, some serious and others not quite as bad.

But Lenihan stressed: "If we had arranged a mid-week game before the last match, we would have been hard pressed to field a team with 15 fit players. We might have been able to but a number of them would have had to play twice that week."

Still, Henry won few friends on the 2001 tour. While the finger of blame may have been pointed at Lenihan when some press conferences were disrupted, he had the easy going personality to be able to deal with the pressure.

While Henry sat in at press conferences apparently in an animated state with not a smile, nod or wink, Lenihan was always capable of throwing out witty one-line responses that more often than not lightened the mood.

Part of Lenihan's brief is to report back to the Four Nations and come up with ideas for improvement in future years.

He has suggested already that future tours may involve less midweek matches in order to allow the players more time for recovery and more time for relaxation.

He is conscious as well that an 11-month season prior to tours of this magnitude and importance does nothing to allow for the proper preparation.

"We have been told that the top English players will now be restricted to something like 32 games each season. Already the Irish Rugby Union have come up with similar proposals and I'm sure that Wales and Scotland will row in.

"But we still have a situation in Europe in 2001/2002 where the European Cup final is scheduled for the end of May and another English final for early June.. If players touring with the Lions are to be given every chance of recovery, they will have to restrict themselves to a limited amount of games, and perhaps we should look at playing those important matches a couple of months before Lions tours are scheduled every four years.

"It is the same every time the Lions tour. Players are involved in big matches right up to leaving. These guys are coming together for the first time and take time to get to know one another while the opposition have generally been playing together for at least a couple of years. They are at a distinct advantage."

For that and other reasons, Lenihan feels these Lions should not be too harshly judged and they probably won't.

"I believe the outcome of the Test series turned on a terrible ten minute spell at the start of the second half of the second game against Australia and on two minutes at the end of the third.

"I am sure the Wallabies were out on their feet at half-time of the second. Had we managed a good start instead of a very bad one, I am positive we would have gone up 2-0 and it would have been all over, done and dusted. Even then, we came agonisingly close."

For all the controversy, sparked by certain sections of the Australian media and spurred on with a large degree of help by untimely and unhelpful comments from the likes of Healey, the Lions were praised for an amount of top class rugby they produced.

Many of the tries were memorable scores and Australia probably still has not recovered from the excitement created by the presence of the thousands of supporters who helped generate unprecedented interest in the Test series.

There had never been anything quite like it before. The sad thing from the Lions point of view is that they lost the series in Australia, and it was the first time that happened in a 102 year history of battle between the Wallabies and Four Nation teams from the northern hemisphere.

But in saying that, Australia and particularly coach Rod Macqueen and captain John Eales deserve the success that came their way. Macqueen retired at the end of the series and Eales called it a day at the conclusion of the Tri Nations in September. It was fitting; no matter how much pain they caused the Lions, that two men of this calibre should bow out of rugby on such a high note. Apart from winning the World Cup, there is no higher honour in rugby.

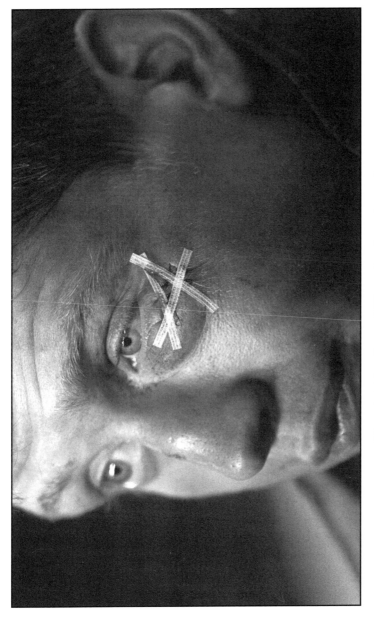

Wounded Lion. Ronan O'Gara sporting a beauty!

The full Irish contingent including Manager Donal Leniha, Baggage Master Pat O'Keeffe and Adminstrative Assistant Joan Moore.

Magic moments for the Irish. Rob Henderson bursts away to set up a try.

Brian O'Driscoll scores at the Gabba.

Keith Wood on the prowl with Australians desperately hanging off him

Daniel Herbert and Stephen Larkham wrap up Henderson.

Read all about it ! Sweet moment after Test in Brisbane !

The face of disappointment.
Rob Henderson and Keith Wood console each other after the series defeat.
Brian O'Driscoll and captain Martin Johnson breathe deeply as they watch
the Wallabies celebrate

CHAPTER 25

PROFILES OF THE LIONS

FULL BACKS

IAIN BALSHSAW (ENGLAND). He started the tour as number one choice ahead of Matt Perry or, at least, that was the presumption. Coach Graham Henry started playing his mind games from day one by choosing Brian O'Driscoll in the number 15 jersey against Western Australia. O'Driscoll, against very weak opposition, did fine, but Balshaw came on as a reserve for the injured Will Greenwood. O'Driscoll moved back to his favourite position in the middle of the field and Balshaw went on to score two magnificent tries. Afterwards, O'Driscoll admitted that he had been awe struck by the Englishman's ability to turn it on. Sadly, from Balshaw's point of view, it all went wrong in the middle of the tour. He lost form, tried too much to make up that lost ground and relinquished his place to his old rival Matt Perry although, of course, he did make cameo appearances in the Test series.

MATT PERRY (ENGLAND). Perry came from "nowhere" to establish himself in the Test side over his Bath club colleague

293

Balshaw. Strangely, he was replaced at half time of the second Test at a time when the Lions led 11-6. Perry was chuffed to learn that he was the only man at that stage not to have been on a losing team to the Wallabies. An Irish journalist, quizzing him about the substitution, reminded Perry that he finished on the winning side in the first Test and was also in a winning position after 40 minutes of the second. "I'll remember that when I run out onto the pitch for the last game," he chuckled. History will show, however, that he didn't have the last laugh he craved for.

WINGS

BEN COHEN (ENGLAND). Perceived to have a good chance of making the Test side. Cohen, however, lost his way early in this tour. Flanker Neil Back berated him for failing to round off a scoring chance in the opening game against Western Australia and he lost the plot again against Australia A. That dismal display cost him dearly, and when he re-discovered form later on it was too late.

DAFFYD JAMES (WALES). He started slowly and did not look Test material early on. Whilst he continued to look one dimensional, his strong running caused problems for opposition defences and he took his try scoring opportunities very well.

DAN LUGER (ENGLAND). Injury prone Luger suffered once again. He fought hard to get himself fit for this tour and did exceptionally well to score four tries in his first two games. Then disaster struck when he damaged his cheekbone in a training ground accident. The injury ended his participation in the tour and the Lions lost a potential match-winner as a result.

JASON ROBINSON (England). Although his defence, particularly his defensive positioning, was occasionally suspect, Robinson lit up this tour with some marvellous running and spectacular tries. The early try he scored in the opening Test was surely the spark the Lions needed. Robinson caused mayhem for the opposition in his six appearances on tour.

*TYRONE HOWE (IRELAND). Howe was absolutely delighted to get the call as a replacement even if he only played one match. He deemed it a great honour and did everything that was required of him against New South Wales Country.

CENTRES

MIKE CATT (ENGLAND). Catt went on tour barely recovered from a back injury and immediately sustained a calf muscle strain. His training was limited but he was allowed stay on tour in the hope of recovery before being forced to appear in the fourth game against Australia A. He didn't last long and limped off and out of the tour without making any real impression.

WILL GREENWOOD (ENGLAND). The strong running Greenwood made a productive contribution until he sustained a leg injury. He hoped against hope but had a huge battle on his hands, particularly when Rob Henderson emerged as the "dark horse" of the tour. He made four appearances but failed to win a Test place due to injury and Henderson's top form.

ROB HENDERSON (IRELAND). Tour manager Donal Lenihan made a bold statement in the middle of the tour when he said Henderson had reinvented himself. On the back of top class displays for Ireland, Henderson was like a runaway train as he bid for a place in the Test side. Set up a crucial try in the opening game against Australia and, despite carrying a knee injury through the latter stages of the second Test and into the third, was one of the stars of the tour.

295

BRIAN O'DRISCOLL (IRELAND). Inevitably, O'Driscoll made the Test side. Inevitably too, he was one of the stars even when the Lions lost. The British and Irish supporters took the well-known Australian "anthem" Waltzing Matilda and re-named it Waltzing O'Driscoll. His try in the first Test will be forever etched in the memory, particularly if the name happens to be Matt Burke, Owen Finegan or Joe Roff plus a half dozen more Wallabies.

MARK TAYLOR (WALES). Taylor had a sound tour and threw down the gauntlet in a couple of matches. Despite his best efforts to win a Test place, he had to fight an uphill and unsuccessful battle because the two Irishmen were in such top form.

*SCOTT GIBBS (Wales). Gibbs was delighted to get the call for the injured Catt and made an immediate impression against New South Wales Country. He didn't play quite as well against ACT when he had a chance to impress on a bigger stage.

OUT HALVES

JONNY WILKINSON (ENGLAND). Wilkinson doesn't have much of a personality. His life revolves around rugby and his second love is cricket. But the work ethic he clings to paid dividends, and his presence was always important to the Lions. Funnily enough, his goal-kicking strike rate wasn't as good as his normal average but he still had an excellent tour.

NEIL JENKINS (WALES). He was a big disappointment and really looked a bit past his sell-by date. The more he tried the more he failed but he still managed to win favour from coach Graham Henry. He was on the bench for the second Test and came on when Wilkinson was carried off near the end. Surprisingly, after showing the Australian attackers the green light, he was again nominated as reserve for the last game but had to cry off through injury.

RONAN O'GARA (IRELAND). O'Gara must still be wondering what he did wrong to deserve being put in the exclusion zone by Henry. Unlike Jenkins, he hardly made a mistake in his four appearances and had a particularly fine game against ACT, one of the most difficult games of the tour. OK, the prospects of pushing Wilkinson out was never an option but he was surely a candidate for the bench and only got the break for the last Test when the coach ran out of options.

SCRUM HALVES

MATT DAWSON (ENGLAND). A star in South Africa back in 1997, Dawson had an indifferent tour for which he appeared to blame everyone but himself. Still, because of injury to Rob Howley, he played some of the second and all of the third Tests.

ROB HOWLEY (WALES). There was genuine delight when Howley was named in the team for the first Test. He lost out through injury in South Africa and believed his chance of making it on this tour was no more than 40-60. But Howley played very well in each and every match and became an automatic choice. The rib injury he sustained in Melbourne was a big blow for him and a bigger one for the Lions.

AUSTIN HEALEY (ENGLAND). Healey became known as "motor-mouth" in the Wallaby camp based on his comments in a weekly column for an English newspaper. His critical descriptions of the Australian people were an absolute disgrace and a PR night-mare for the Lions. The timing, let alone the wording, of his com-ments on Australian second row Justin Harrison gave the Wallabies the stick they needed to bash the Lions with in the cru-cial third Test. For all that, he was good on the pitch and remained one of Henry's favourite players, if not people.

297

*ANDY NICOL (SCOTLAND). One can't say much, if anything about Nicol. He was on holiday in Australia and was brought into the 22-man squad when Howley and Healey were ruled out of the third Test. He never saw any action.

PROPS

DARREN MORRIS (WALES). He saw ten minutes of Test action in Sydney but really made little impact on the tour. Tom Smith retained his place on the side after featuring strongly on the winning side in South Africa and Jason Leonard came on as a substitute in the opening two Tests, once as a loose head for Smith and then on the other side for Phil Vickery.

JASON LEONARD (ENGLAND). Anyone who ever felt the English are arrogant could never point the finger at Leonard who is a charming man – proof that you can be successful and nice at the same time. He reckoned the chances of securing a Test place were poor but got on with the job in hand. When he didn't make the starting side he never complained and was rewarded for his loyalty with appearances in Tests one and two.

TOM SMITH (SCOTLAND). Smith doesn't make much noise or much of a fuss about things. The speculators figured he would lose his place in the Test side but Smith had other ideas from the start. Quietly and efficiently, Smith set about removing any doubt about his ability and he enjoyed a productive tour.

PHIL VICKERY (ENGLAND). His work rate around the field was immense but there was always a nagging doubt about his scrummaging ability. He was particularly troubled in that area during the second Test and was replaced by Leonard as a result. Still, he had a decent tour.

DAVID YOUNG (WALES). A controversial enough choice, Young appeared to struggle at times. His strengths, however, were his leadership abilities and the experience that went with it. He became the regular midweek captain and was also very supportive of the Test side and the party as a whole.

HOOKERS

KEITH WOOD (IRELAND). An inspiration in South Africa in 1997, Wood was similarly lauded for his performances in Australia. An Irish photographer declared that it was almost impossible to keep the Irishman out of his photographs. "He seemed to appear in every frame I took," he said. He was hailed by the print media and by TV and radio commentators for his performances in the Tests, even when things did not go the way of the Lions. Sadly, he has decided he won't be available for the Lions tour to New Zealand in 2005.

PHIL GREENING (ENGLAND). A training ground accident in the early stages was enough to rule the competitive Greening out of the tour and he never even got to wear the prized Lions shirt.

ROBIN MCBRYDE (WALES). The step-up from international rugby with Wales to the Lions proved a little too much for McBryde. He struggled badly against Australia A, came on as a substitute against New South Wales and made no further appearances, partially because of injury.

***GORDON BULLOCH** (SCOTLAND). He was unlucky not to have made the original tour party and replaced Greening early on. Made a cameo appearance in the opening Test as a blood replacement for Wood but never played well enough to launch a serious challenge.

*DORIAN WEST (ENGLAND). It was a bad tour for hookers, Wood apart, and West took advantage when called out for McBryde. He played well against ACT and must have also impressed in training because he was named on the bench for the final Test.

SECOND ROWS

JEREMY DAVIDSON (IRELAND). He was surely disappointed at failing to hold onto the Test place he commanded in 1997. This was, however, an area of fierce competition with four locks going for one place alongside captain Martin Johnson. He hardly put a foot wrong but needed just a little more to press his claims.

MALCOLM O'KELLY (IRELAND). The tallest player in the party was given a sporting chance of making the Test side at the start. A lack-lustre display in difficult circumstances against Australia A was enough to damage that potential. On such a short tour, O'Kelly had no real opportunity to make up lost ground.

SCOTT MURRAY (SCOTLAND). A similar type player to O'Kelly, Murray will hardly thank coach Henry for picking them as partners for the Australia A match. Murray was very disappointing in that fixture and suffered with the Irishman as a result.

DANNY GREWCOCK (ENGLAND). While other candidates failed to take their chances, Grewcock certainly made the most of his. He was more influential than most forwards on the tour and fully deserved his place in the Test games in which he enhanced his reputation.

MARTIN JOHNSON (ENGLAND). Johnson is not the most talkative of people but he had the support of the players at all stages of the tour. He was a major influence up to the last two Tests but then seemed to lose the plot a bit.. Certainly, he was not the dominant force one had come to expect and the Lions suffered out of touch in those crucial matches. The ultimate insult to Johnson was when Justin Harrison snaffled possession in the last line out of the match from under Johnson's nose – on a Lions throw – in Sydney.

FLANKERS

NEIL BACK (ENGLAND). He picked up an injury in advance of the first Test but came back for the second and scored a try. He was not as influential as usual in the last two matches although, overall, he had a good tour.

COLIN CHARVIS (WALES). Banned for a week when the Lions had to play ACT and the second Test, Charvis had the right to feel aggrieved at the punishment. He had a reasonable if unspectacular tour and finished by making a 40-minute appearance in the third Test as substitute for Scott Quinnell.

LAWRENCE DALLAGLIO (ENGLAND). He made no serious impact on this tour because of the knee injury he tried to shake off. His first game was in the fourth match against Australia A and he played again against New South Wales before finally admitting defeat in his battle with injury.

RICHARD HILL (ENGLAND). He had a superb tour and was a major influence until a cheap shot by Wallaby centre Nathan Gray ended his tour. Ruled out with concussion, Hill was replaced by Martin Corry for the remainder of the Test series.

SIMON TAYLOR (SCOTLAND). Scored a try in the opening match with Western Australia but the 21 year old "rookie" was injured in that game and was back home before he knew it.

MARTIN WILLIAMS (WALES). Williams was more workmanlike than spectacular. He never gave less than 100 per cent but that was never enough to get him the Lions Test cap he sought. Instead, he had to be happy with a supporting role on the bench.

*MARTIN CORRY (ENGLAND). When he joined the tour as replacement for Taylor, he made an immediate impact. His selection didn't please English coach Clive Woodward who had to plan without him for a tour game against Canada, but Corry made the most of his chance. He played a big role in the first Test, was unlucky to be dropped for the second but then came on to replace the injured Hill and hold his place for the third game. Even in the series defeat, Corry was highly impressive.

*DAVID WALLACE (IRELAND). Barely off the plane, Wallace made his first appearance against New South Wales Country and then went on to have a big outing against ACT, a match in which he scored a try. He might well have pushed Neil Back if he had just a little more time and more matches. Instead, he had to be happy with those two appearances and a free holiday towards the end of the tour.

NUMBER EIGHT

SCOTT QUINNELL (WALES). Those who doubted Quinnell's ability to last the pace were proven very wrong. The big, bustling Welshman was one of the most consistent players on the tour and was always ready to put his body on the line for the cause.

* Replacement player.

APPENDICES

APPENDIX A
2001 LIONS RECORD AT A GLANCE

Played	Won	Drew	Lost	For	Against
10	7	0	3	449	184

Western Australia	W	116-10
Queensland Presidents	W	83-6
Queensland	W	42-8
Australia A	L	25-28
New South Wales	W	41-24
New South Wales Country	W	46-3
AUSTRALIA	W	29-13
ACT	W	30-28
AUSTRALIA	L	14-35
AUSTRALIA	L	23-29

APPENDIX B
INDIVIDUAL SCORING

Player	Tries	Conversions	Penalties	Drop Goals	Total.
Jonny Wilkinson	2	13	12	0	72
Jason Robinson	10	0	0	0	50
Neil Jenkins	0	10	4	0	32
Ronan O'Gara	0	13	0	0	26
Matt Dawson	0	6	3	0	21
Dan Luger	4	0	0	0	20
Austin Healey	4	0	0	0	20
Brian O'Driscoll	4	0	0	0	20
Rob Henderson	4	0	0	0	20
Scott Quinnell	4	0	0	0	20
Colin Charvis	3	0	0	0	15
Daffyd James	3	0	0	0	15
Neil Back	3	0	0	0	15
Matt Perry	1	4	0	0	13
Rob Howley	2	0	0	0	10
Iain Balshaw	2	0	0	0	10
Mark Taylor	2	0	0	0	10
David Young	2	0	0	0	10
Ben Cohen	2	0	0	0	10
Simon Taylor	1	0	0	0	5
Will Greenwood	1	0	0	0	5
Danny Grewcock	1	0	0	0	5
Malcolm O'Kelly	1	0	0	0	5
Richard Hill	1	0	0	0	5
Scott Gibbs	1	0	0	0	5
David Wallace	1	0	0	0	5
PENALTY TRY	1	0	0	0	5
Total	60	46	19	0	449

Gordon Bulloch, Mike Catt, Martin Corry, Lawrence Dallaglio, Jeremy Davidson, Phil Greening, Tyrone Howe, Martin Johnson, Jason Leonard, Robin McBryde, Darren Morris, Scott Murray, Tom Smith, Phil Vickery, Dorian West, Martyn Williams, Keith Wood and Andy Nicol did not score.

The Lions conceded 184 points made up of 18 tries, 26 penalties and 8 conversions.

APPENDIX C
INDIVIDUAL PLAYING RECORDS

Player	WA	QP	REDS	AUS A	NSW	NSW C	1st TEST	ACT	2nd TEST	3rd TEST
Back, Neil	7 2t	7		7	7				7 1t	7
Balshaw, Iain	R13 2t		15	15	15	15	R15	15	R15	R14
Bulloch, Gordon		R2		R2		2	R2	R2		
Catt, Mike				13						
Charvis, Colin		6 2t	R7	R8		6 1t	R7			R8
Cohen, Ben	14			11		14 2t		14		
Corry, Martin		8	8		R	8	6	8	R6	6
Dallagio, Lawrence				6	6					
Davidson, Jeremy	R4	4		R5				4		
Dawson, Matt		9	R9	R9 2c	9 1c			9 2c 2p	R9	9
Gibbs, Scott						12, 1t		12		
Greening, Phil										
Greenwood, Will	13 1t	13		13	12					
Grewcock, Danny	4 1t		5		5		5		5	5
Healey, Austin	R9 1t	R10		9		9 1t		11 2t		
Henderson, Rob	R14	12 3t	12 1t				12		12	12
Hill, Richard	6		6 1t		R		7	6		
Howe, Tyrone						11		R		
Howley, Rob	9 2t		9				9		9	
James, Dafydd		14	14 1t		14 1t		14 1t	R13	14	14
Jenkins, Neil		10 5c		10 2p		10 5c 2p			R10	
Johnson, Martin		4 *		4 *			4 *		4 *	* 4
Leonard, Jason	R3	R1		1		1	R1	R1	R3	
Luger, Dan	11 3t		11 1t							
McBryde, Robin	R2	2		2						
Morris, Darren	1			R3		R1		1		R1
Murray, Scott		5	R4	4		R		5		
Nicol, Andy										
O'Driscoll, Brian	15 1t		13 1t		13 1t		13 1t		13	13
O'Gara, Ronan	10 13c				R10	R12		10		
O'Kelly, Malcolm	5	R4 1t		5		5		R		
Perry, Matt		15 4c		15 1t	R		15		15	15
Quinnell, Scott	8 3t			8	8		8 1t		8	8
Robinson, Jason		11 5t		14 1t	11 2t		11 1t		11	11 1t
Smith, Tom		1	1				1		1	1
Taylor, Mark	12 1t	R13		R12 1t		13		13		
Taylor, Simon	R6 1t									
Vickery, Phil	3	3					3		3	3
Wallace, David						R		61t		
West, Dorian								2		
Wilkinson, Jonny			10 4c 3p		10 1t 3c 2p		10 3c 1p		10 3p	10 1t 3p 2c
Williams, Martyn		7		7		7		7		
Wood, Keith	2 *		2	2		2		2	2	2
Young, David		3 * 1t		3 *		3* 1t		3*		

Key: t - try; c- conversion; P - penalty goal; Number- player's position; R - Replacement (and player replaced); * - captain

306

APPENDIX D
LIONS RECORDS

Team Records in a Test Match

Highest Score for: 31-0 v Australia (1966)

Biggest Win: 31-0 v Australia

Highest Score Against: 38 v New Zealand (1983)

Worst Loss: 32 points (6-38) v New Zealand

Player Records in a Test Match

Most points

For: 18 - Tony Ward v South Africa 1980
             Gavin Hastings v New Zealand 1983
             Jonny Wilkinson v Australia 2001.

Against: 25 - Matt Burke (Australia) Second Test 2001

Player Records in a Test Series

Most Points

For: 41 – Neil Jenkins v South Africa 1997

Against: 46 – Allan Hewson (New Zealand) 1983

Players Records in a Career (in Tests)

Most Points

For: 66- Gavin Hastings (6 appearances)
Against: 46 – Allan Hewson (4 appearances)

Most Tries

For: 10 – Tony O'Reilly (10 appearances)
Against: 5 – Frank Mitchinson (New Zealand 3 appearances)
          5 – Theuns Briers (South Africa – 4 appearances)

Touring Match Records

Highest Score
116-10 v Western Australia 2001

Biggest Win
106 points against Western Australia.

Highest Score Conceded
39 points (W 67-39) v Northern Free State 1997

Most Tries Scored
18 v Western Australia 2001

Most Tries Conceded
8 v Victoria (W 41-36) 1930.

Player Records on a Tour

Most Points
188 – Barry John in Australia/New Zealand 1971 (17 appearances)

Most Tries
30 – Randolph Aston in South Africa 1891.

Player Records in a Career (all Matches)

Most Points
281 – Andy Irvine

Most Tries
38 - Tony O'Reilly.

APPENDIX E
THE IRISH RUGBY TOURISTS

R. Alexander (NIFC) 1938
W.J. Ashby (UCC) 1910

G. Beamish (Leicester, RAF) 1930
C.A.Boyd (Trinity) 1896
C.V. Boyle (Trinity) 1938
M.J. Bradley (Dolphin) 1924
T.N. Brand (NIFC) 1924
B. Bresnihan (UCD) 1966/1968
N. Brophy (Blackrock) 1959/1962
L. Bulger (Lansdowne) 1896

N. Carr (Ards) 1986*
O. Campbell (Old Belvedere) 1980/1983
T. Clifford (Young Munster) 1950
A.D. Clinch (Wanderers) 1896
J. Clinch (Wanderers) 1924
T. Crean (Wanderers) 1896
G.E.Cromey (Queens) 1938
V. Cunningham (St. Mary's) 1993
W. Cunningham (Lansdowne) 1924

I.G. Davidson (NIFC) 1903
J. Davidson (London Irish/Castres) 1997/2001
P. Dean (St. Mary's) 1989
R. Dawson (Wanderers) 1959
G.P. Doran (Lansdowne) 1899
M. Doyle (Blackrock) 1968

W. Duggan (Blackrock) 1977
M.J.Dunne (Lansdowne) 1904

M. English (Bohemian) 1959
R.W. Edwards (Malone) 1904

J.L. Farrell (Bective) 1930
C. Fitzgerald (St Mary's) 1983
D. Fitzgerald (Lansdowne) 1986*
A.R.Foster (Derry) 1910

M. Galwey (Shannon) 1993
M. Gibson (Cambridge University/NIFC) 1966/68/71/74/77.
K. Goodall (Derry) 1968
T. Grace (St. Mary's) 1974
C.R. Graves (Wanderers) 1938

N. Henderson (Queens) 1950
R. Henderson (Wasps) 2001
D. Hewitt (Queens) 1959/1962
M. Hipwell (Terenure) 1971
T. Howe (Dungannon) 2001
W. Hunter (CIYMS) 1962

D. Irwin (Instonians) 1983

R. Johnston (Wanderers) 1896

M. Keane (Lansdowne) 1977
K. Kennedy (CIYMS/London Irish) 1966/1974
M. Kiernan (Dolphin) 1983/1986**
T.J. Kiernan (UCC/Cork Constitution) 1962/1968

J. Kyle (Queens) 1950

R. Lamont (Instonians) 1966
M. Lane (UCC) 1950
D. Lenihan (Cork Constitution) 1983 / 1986* / 1989
S. Lynch (St. Mary's) 1971

J. Magee (Bective) 1896
L. Magee (Bective) 1896
H. MacNeill (Blackrock) 1983
E. Martelli (Trinity) 1899
B.S. Masey (Hull / Ulster) 1904
R.B. Mayne (Queens) 1938
W.J.McBride (Ballymena) 1962 / 66 / 68 / 71 / 74
J. McCarthy (Dolphin) 1950
A.N.McClinton (NIFC) 1910
T.N.McGown (NIFC) 1899
B. McKay (Queens) 1950
H. McKibbin (Queens) 1938
S. McKinney (Dungannon) 1974
G. McLoughlin (Shannon) 1983
R. McLoughlin (Gosforth / Blackrock) 1966 / 1971
J.V. McVicker (Collegians) 1924
A.D. Meares (Trinity) 1896
E. Millar (Leicester) 1997
S. Millar (Ballymena) 1959 / 1962 / 1968
D. Milliken (Bangor) 1974
J. Moloney (St. Mary's) 1974
G.J. Morgan (Clontarf) 1938
B. Mulcahy (UCD / Bohemian / Bective) 1959 / 1962
K. Mullen (Old Belvedere) 1950
A Mulligan (Wanderers / London Irish) 1959

B Mullin (Blackrock) 1986*/1989
N. Murphy (Cork Constitution) 1959/1966
P.F. Murray (Wanderers) 1930

J Nelson (Malone) 1950
G Norton (Bective) 1950

R O'Donnell (St. Mary's) 1980
B O'Driscoll (Blackrock) 2001
J. O'Driscoll (London Irish/Manchester) 1980/1983
R O'Gara (Cork Constitution) 2001
M. O'Kelly (St. Mary's) 2001
H O'H O'Neill (Queens) 1930
T O'Reilly (Old Belvedere) 1955/1959
P Orr (Old Wesley) 1977/1980

C D. Patterson (Malone) 1904
C Patterson (Instonians) 1980
C Pedlow (Queens) 1955
O J S Piper (Cork Constitution) 1910
N. Popplewell (Greystones) 1993

T. Reid (Garryowen) 1955
J. Robbie (Greystones) 1980
R. Roe (Lansdowne) 1955
W.J. Roche (UCC/Newport) 1924
T. Ringland (Ballymena) 1983/1986*

J.W. Sealy (Trinity) 1896
F Slatery (Blackrock) 1971/1974
S Smith (Ballymena) 1989
R S Smyth (Trinity) 1903

T. Smyth (Newport) 1910

A Tedford (Malone) 1903
R Thompson (Instonians) 1955
C Tucker (Shannon) 1980
W Tyrrell (Queens) 1910

S Walker (Instonians) 1955
D Wallace (Garryowen) 2001
James Wallace (Wanderers) 1903
Joseph Wallace (Wanderers) 1903
P Wallace (Saracens) 1997
R Wallace (Garryowen) 1993
J Walsh (Sunday's Well) 1966
T Ward (Garryowen) 1980
G. Wood (Garryowen) 1959
K. Wood (Harlequins) 1997/2001
R. Young (Queens) 1966/1968

* Denotes appearance against The Rest of the World in Cardiff
** Denotes place in the squad against The Rest of the World.

CAPTAINS
1910 – Tom Smith
1938 – Sammy Walker
1950 – Karl Mullen
1955 – Robin Thompson
1959 – Ronnie Dawson
1968 – Tom Kiernan
1974 - Willie John McBride
1983 – Ciaran Fitzgerald

MANAGERS

1955 - Jack Siggins
1966 – Des O'Brien
1980 – Syd Millar
1983 – Willie John McBride
2001 - Donal Lenihan

ASSISTANT MANAGERS

1962 – Harry McKibbin
1974 – Syd Millar
1980 – Noel Murphy

COACHES

1968 – Ronnie Dawson
1974 – Syd Millar
1980 - Noel Murphy
1986 – Mick Doyle (v Rest of World).